you are not alone

imani

Copyright © 2008 imani

All rights reserved.

No part of this book may be reproduced,
stored in a retrieval system, or transmitted
in any form or by any means
without prior written consent.

ISBN: 1-4392-1611-8

ISBN-13: 9781439216118

Visit www.booksurge.com to order additional copies.

you are not alone

"Regardless of your spiritual beliefs, *You Are Not Alone* will faithfully serve as a trusted companion: it is truly a magnanimous book. . . imani's breathtaking sincerity and most importantly her faith in those unexpected 5 a.m. meetings with God, offer both insight and inspiration to all."

– **M.T. Hoashi, Author of** *The Tea Master's Son*

"Not since *Acts of Faith* have I read a book that speaks to my every day life. There's something in this book for everyone. Questions, answers, and a calm knowing that none of us are in this alone. . . You'll truly find yourself wishing that it didn't have to end."

– **Travis Hunter, Best-selling Author of** *The Hearts of Men*

"In *You Are Not Alone*, Author imani invites the reader on her own journey of introspection, self-discovery and intimate God-moments to provoke the same life-changing experience. The wisdom and spiritual insight together with the transparent vulnerability make reading this book more than pleasurable. It's a must read for anyone trying to live their best life."

– **Sherri L. Lewis, Best-selling Author of**
My Soul Cries Out **and** *Dance Into Destiny*

"Is it possible for just one book to inspire you, bring you to tears of gratitude and joy, hug you when you're down, make you giggle, *and* get you moving? *You Are Not Alone* does just that. This book is like a daily dose of encouragement straight from one of God's messengers."

– **Monica Parker, Author of** *The Unhappy Lawyer:*
A Roadmap to Finding Meaningful Work Outside of the Law

This book is dedicated to my role model, Tamara. Your eternal optimism and insatiable passion for life never cease to amaze me.

Preface

It's no accident that you're holding this book.

If you've picked it up, it's because there's something in these pages just for you. Maybe an answer to something you've been struggling with, or maybe just the comfort of knowing that someone else out there has the same questions, doubts, struggles, hopes, and dreams as you do.

Since this isn't a typical self-help book, maybe I should tell you a little bit about how it came to be. I think it's important you understand that I'm not a minister or spiritual guru; not even someone who set out to write about my quiet time with God. I'm just a girl who had a dream.

It all started several years ago, when I decided that I wanted to write a book. I wanted to be the next great fiction writer and climb up the best-sellers lists. In fact, I spent countless hours at local bookstores and coffee shops waiting for that magical idea to strike. After all, isn't that what happens? People know what their purpose is and set out to fulfill it, right?

Maybe that happens to some folks, but not me. Instead, I kind of side stepped into mine.

When the best-selling fiction idea didn't quickly materialize, I decided to pray for God to show me my story in a dream. Yeah, it sounded kind of kooky, even to me. But, I figured nothing else had worked, so why not give it a try? That night I dreamed that I should write about my life. If you've ever prayed about your purpose, you can imagine how excited I was to have a clue. The only problem was that nothing particularly exciting had ever happened to me.

Then, bam! A few weeks later my seemingly perfect world fell apart. I lost my husband and a lifetime of dreams in an instant. I began to write for my own healing, then slowly but surely learned that my story could inspire others.

When I finished writing *When I Was Broken*, I was spent! I'd exposed my worst moments, and wanted nothing more than to put it behind me and move on to my true calling – writing fiction.

Have you ever heard the saying, "Man makes plans and God laughs?" Well, in my case, it's true. I planned to write fiction, but God had something else in mind.

A few months ago I found myself praying about my second book as I was running on a track near my house. While running, I had the most exhilarating experience. It was like my feet were moving without me, and I felt as if I could have run for days. I felt as if God was telling me that if I got up at 5 a.m. to write each morning, he'd give me the right topic and words.

That day I ran 5 miles.

Let me pause one moment to make sure you understand the significance of this moment.

First, "runner" is not a term anyone would use to describe me. I'm guessing that a really old lady could pass me on the track without getting winded, and that by the time she got warmed up, I would have finished my short workout and made it back home. In other words, the fact that I ran 5 miles without stopping was beyond incredible.

Second, you'll notice that instead of going to church, I was out on a track running. Why? Because, despite my strong Christian upbringing, I wasn't exactly part of the front pew committee.

Third, sleep is one of a handful of things I love most in the world. Needless to say, getting up at 5 a.m. seemed absurd. Absolutely ridiculous!

Finally, even if I believed that God would give me the words to write (which I admit to seriously doubting) I really didn't want to write this book because I have a love-hate relationship with self-help books. I buy them, and *if* I read them, I usually get a nugget that I can use. But, most often they stay on my shelf unread because half of the book usually tells me something I already know, and the other half typically repeats those same points until I'm ready to scream "I've got it already!" (Actually, the original title of this book was *I Hate Self-Help Books*.)

With that backdrop, it should come as no surprise that when my alarm went off the day after my run, I quickly convinced myself I'd been delusional and no good could come from getting up at such an "ungodly" hour.

But, here's when I knew without a shadow of a doubt that there is a God, and that he has a HUGE sense of humor. A few weeks later I began waking up at 5 a.m. without an alarm, with no rhyme or reason. As a person who loves sleep, I was beside myself!

Finally, almost out of desperation, I started praying and journaling early in the morning. Sometimes I wouldn't even get out of bed; I'd just pull the laptop close and write whatever came to my spirit. I wrote questions to God about my hopes, dreams, and disappointments; and marveled over the answers that came in response. I didn't stop to second guess or edit; I just typed as quickly as I could so that I could go back to sleep and be done.

Later in the day, I'd read over the passage – often with surprise at what it said because I had no real memory of writing it. Then, although the passages were often quite personal, I began emailing them to a friend or two. The first few times I emailed them just in the spirit of sharing, but soon thereafter, something truly amazing happened.

Friends, and friends of friends who were forwarded my thoughts, requested that I add them to my distribution list. Then, those same individuals began to tell me that messages reached them at the exact right moment because of something they were going through. Slowly, but surely, my distribution list began to grow and this "thing" began to take shape. I was (and am still) amazed!

It was exciting, inspiring, humbling, and quite scary all at the same time. I found myself wondering how long I would be a 5 a.m. writer, how long I'd have things to write about, and how I'd keep my focus on what was most important – my quiet time with God. Even then I don't think I realized this "thing" was to be my second book.

Needless to say, this isn't your typical self-help book that tells you what you're doing wrong and how to do it better. This is just a journal of a girl who hopes that by sharing her own challenges and lessons, someone else might be comforted.

In compiling these pieces, I've been so tempted to pull out the editing tools and group the thoughts in a way that makes more organizational sense. But, in the end, I resisted. This book isn't about how well I can (or can't) write or how well I can organize. In fact, it isn't about me at all. That's why these writings are almost exactly as I originally wrote them during those early morning hours. Of course that shouldn't stop you from following your own spirit as you read. You can read in the order in which they were written, or you can just pick a topic that feels right to you that day.

So, here it is – moments of triumph and vulnerabilities. Times when I found perfect peace and days when I prayed to get through the moment. On the pages that follow, I offer you myself and my discussions with God, unedited. I hope this will remind you that no matter what you've experienced or what challenges come your way, YOU ARE NOT ALONE.

Peace, blessings, and love to you all,

imani

"imani" means faith, and everything I write is by faith

Contents

- Change· 1
- Prayer· 5
- Loneliness· 9
- Peace· 13
- Purpose· 17
- Loss· 21
- Faith· 27
- Confidence· 31
- Obstacles To Your Purpose· 35
- Disappointment· 39
- Joy· 45
- Discipline· 49
- Ego· 53
- Agape Love· 59
- The Illusion Of Control· 63
- Being In The Moment· 67
- The Cocoon· 71
- Me· 75
- Progress· 81
- Obedience· 87
- Our Thoughts· 91
- Hope· 95
- Supply and Demand· 99
- Adaptation· 103
- Our Path· 107

The Rain	113
Miracles	117
Putting First Things First	119
Angels	123
Being Plugged In	127
Lack	131
One Day At A Time	135
Addiction	139
Love	143
Now	145
Letting Go	149
The Between Time	153
Sharing	157
Being Still	161
A Sense Of Belonging	163
A Truce	165
Happily Ever After	169
The Mirror	171
The Ups and Downs	173
Answers to Prayers	177
Believing In Dreams	181
Stepping Out	185
Wanting More	187
Waiting On Prayers To Be Answered	191
Keeping On	195
Feeling Alone	197

What About Change?

I could tell you what it's like on the other side. But, that would be like trying to describe to a caterpillar what life will be like as a butterfly. Can't you imagine the butterfly saying, "For real, you're going to be SO much more beautiful! And happy! And free! I'm telling you, you're going to be able to fly and everything!"

The caterpillar, who's either crawling around on a tree stump, or worse, stuck somewhere in a cocoon wondering what the heck just happened, saying, "I'm going to be like you? Well, exactly how is that going to happen? And, how long do I have to wait?" Or, my all time favorite – and yes we've all been crazy enough to think it: "What if I don't want to be a butterfly? What if I just want to be a caterpillar?"

Have you ever felt that way? Like you knew your challenges were preparing you to do and be better, but yet you still wanted things to go back to the way they were?

Yeah, that's the real crazy part, because it makes absolutely no logical sense when you think about it. Name one good reason why a caterpillar would choose to stay a little insect with nothing else going for it but the infinite number of legs that it needs when traveling at .000000000000001 miles per hour from tree to tree.

I'm still waiting.

Yet, I've been there. I've been so entrenched in my comfort zone that being a caterpillar was the only thing I could perceive.

You want to know what else? The thought of flying scared the heebeegeebees out of me. I didn't see it as something beautiful and liberating. I saw it as one of the most terrifying possibilities for the future. I saw it as different, uncertain, and unnecessary.

I didn't want to change.

Why? Because I had a vision for my future that didn't include flying all around the world as some jet-setting butterfly. No sirree. I was comfortable right where I was, crawling. In fact, I was going to be the best crawler I could be. I had it all figured out.

Which is why I was so thrown when I woke up one day in a cocoon. Which is why I started using all of my might – kicking and screaming for someone to let me out; and growing mad when God seemed to turn a deaf ear.

It's dark. It's lonely. I can't see, so I'm scared all of the time. I long for the days when I can see light again, but at the same time I'm scared to death of what will happen then.

After all, what if I can't crawl anymore? What then?

Who's going to teach me how to fly? Be with me if I fall? Tell me that I'm beautiful?

Nope it's settled. I don't want to be a butterfly. God please just let me stay a caterpillar where it's safe!

I'm happy here. . . . Except, that's the thing. I'm really NOT happy here.

If I'm honest with myself, being a caterpillar has its limitations. And, being in a cocoon just flat out sucks.

Can we ever be happy – truly happy – as less than what God made us to be? Knowing that we're destined for something bigger and better, can we find contentment if we settle for less than?

I don't think so. Even if it's sometimes scary, uncomfortable, and uncertain; I think we owe it to ourselves to grow and change in ways that will be infinitely better for us in the end.

God, help me to remember that the cocoons of life are temporary, and that when I emerge from this place, I will be infinitely better, stronger, and more beautiful than ever before.

What About Prayer?

There are times when I get down on my knees and wonder why I even bother.

Have you ever felt that way? Like your prayers didn't change anything? Like God was listening, then proceeding with business as usual?

Don't even try to act like you don't feel me. You know that at some point in your life you've felt that way too. You've prayed the same prayer for the 100th time and started to wonder if anyone was listening. Not saying that you doubted the existence of God; just saying perhaps you wondered why bother asking when it seems as if he's going to do what he wants regardless?

I can remember a time when I was down on my knees praying and I literally felt like I couldn't get up if God didn't change my situation. I was praying and crying – it was really quite dramatic in hindsight – because I actually remember telling God, "I'm not doing this anymore! You're going to have to work something out here, because I'm tired of being patient! No more!"

I wanted God to miraculously heal my then husband of the mental illness that had fallen upon him and then restore my marriage, despite the infidelity and lies that had torn it apart. I kept praying about what I wanted, and waiting – somewhat patiently – for God to fix it in the manner in which I'd decided was best. Then, when days turned into weeks and weeks turned into months, I got fed up. So, I got big and bad and TOLD God I wasn't doing it anymore. I'd been patient and faithful, and it was time for him to come through on his part of the bargain.

I'm laughing at the thought of it now. In hindsight, I'm amazed at my boldness. But, at the time, it seemed like a perfectly reasonable ultimatum. "God, either you fix this situation right now, or I'm gonna . . . ." Yeah, there was a slight glitch in my plan. How do you threaten God? "I'm gonna stop believing in You?" Yeah, that would fix him! "I'm gonna end my life?" Whoo-hooo, that would really show him. I mean, really, how does one *make* God do anything?

Nonetheless, that's what I told him. I was tired of being stuck in that situation, and it was time for God to fix it.

I sat there rocking, praying, crying, and begging in a way that you'll only understand if you've ever been "through." Then, I waited for something to happen. After all, that's the power of prayer, right?

I waited for my then husband to walk back into the room in his right mind and somehow magically wipe all of our marital problems away. I waited for the situation to resolve in the way in which I'd fantasized.

But it didn't.

My husband kept talking to people who weren't there. I had to deal with the reality of my marriage ending, and the insecurities that come from being cheated on. Not to mention the shame that I shouldn't have felt, but that comes when you care too much about what other people think.

My situation didn't change.

But, a real miracle did happen that day. Because the more I rocked, prayed, cried, and begged; the more God began to come into my heart and fill me with His peace. As the peace filled me, I realized my prayer wasn't what I thought it was. I thought I wanted to go back to the way things were before. I thought I couldn't make it "through" the hard times to a place of healing.

But really, I just didn't feel like I could do it alone.

I knew that if I could make it through, I might be better for having gone through the trial. I would love harder, take less for granted, become more secure than I'd ever been. Some part of me knew there was no going back – only forward. I was just scared because I didn't think I was strong enough to make it.

When God answered my prayer by being there with me, holding me, comforting me, and loving me in the way that only he could; my situation didn't change, but I did.

Just that easily, I finally understood the reason for prayer.

What About Loneliness?

Have you ever been lonely? I mean, the kind of loneliness that you feel physically – like an aching down deep in your soul?

I have. I've been in a crowded room of people who loved me, yet felt as if I was all alone. And, more times than I care to admit, I've prayed that God would end the loneliness by bringing me the man who I'm supposed to be with forever. Since I've been married, I figure that I might have to get back in line behind my single girlfriends who've never been married before, but otherwise, it shouldn't take too long, right?

Wrong.

Seven years – seven long years – after my divorce, and I'm still single. Wondering who this person is and what life she's living. "She" was supposed to be happily married with 2 or 3 kids, her own business, and lots of community service. She was supposed to be part of the PTA and carpool, and be exchanging tips on good schools and extra-curricular activities.

She wasn't supposed to be all alone. And, worse yet, sometimes lonely.

Sometimes, when I'm thinking like this, I feel so deeply that there's something missing. I want to grab hold of something *or someone* to fill it. (I must admit that in the past, I have!) I find myself daydreaming about that special someone, and thinking if "he" was here, it would all be okay.

But if I'm real with myself, I'll admit that as long as I'm trying to fill a gaping hole, I'm really not ready. Because if he comes along while that hole is there, he'll just fall right through it. Plus, I'll still have a void.

Those of us who are single have got to stop thinking that he'll come along and make everything right. Also, those of us in relationships have got to stop looking to our mates as our ultimate savior. We can't expect any person to complete us. Instead, "he" takes good and makes it better, or better and makes it best. He doesn't take brokenness and make it whole. He complements, not completes us.

On the other hand, HE takes us beyond brokenness. HE is our ultimate source of everything we need. HE doesn't mind that we're imperfect and insecure; HE doesn't judge. HE never tires of our long rambling stories and never needs space when we want to cuddle. HE's always supportive and tells us we're beautiful on what we think is our worst day. HE always sleeps over and waits around for breakfast. Plus I'm always more than enough for HIM – even if I think I'm too skinny or weigh too much, talk more than I should or am extremely shy, when I feel as if I don't always fit in . . . . HE loves me just the way I am.

What's even better is HE promised to love me forever and I don't have to wonder if he means it.

Next time it seems so tempting to fill the void with "him," I think I'll give HIM a try instead. It doesn't mean that I'll stop praying for my soulmate. But maybe, just maybe, it means that I'll actually be ready when he comes.

What About Peace?

I'm not sleepy.

That in and of itself may not sound incredible, except that it's 5 am and I've only gotten 4 hours of sleep so far. Add on to that the fact that I absolutely love sleep and have never been a morning person. Yet, here I am up at 5 (having woken up without an alarm), anxiously waiting for the familiar excitement that wells up inside of me when I'm inspired to write a nugget for the day.

The hotel room I'm in (because I'm traveling for work) is quiet, except for the humming of the heater. It's also dark, except for the light from my blackberry. There's a stillness that the early morning brings that makes me think I understand instinctively why God designated this "ungodly" hour for our writing time. It's the only time of day when I'm not in some way distracted by all of the seemingly important things that consume my day.

Will I get the project finished in time? Do I even care? Is my mom ok? Is today the day when I get a book deal? Will he (whoever "he" of the day is) call? Or maybe I should call him? Is a better him coming soon? What should I eat for lunch/dinner/snack? Is today the day when something miraculous will happen? If not today, then when? When?

These gazillion thoughts consume me, overwhelm me, and in some odd way even comfort me because it's the familiar, from the time my alarm goes off at its normal 8:00 a.m. time, until I reluctantly drift off to sleep after midnight.

Wow. God couldn't find time in my schedule as it was, so he made us a new one. That thought makes me laugh out loud because it's true.

Last Saturday he tried to find a moment with me – made it so that my cell phone wouldn't dial out and somehow took away battery charge on the blackberry I had plugged up all night. What did I do? So desperate to fill the moments, I tried everything before finally hitting pay dirt. My text messaging still worked! Yes!

Why was I so afraid of the quiet time with God, that I'd literally almost taken my phone apart to make a way to talk to someone (anyone – because mind you I didn't have a specific call to make) rather than be alone with my thoughts? Why?

Have you ever resisted those quiet moments?

If I'm honest with myself and you, I think it's because time alone with God seems like time in front of the mirror. When it's just me and him, I think I'll see myself more clearly; and, let me just say that I don't always like what I see.

So, I resist. Because I think time with him is going to be like it is when I look in my own mirror. I'm going to see the broken places and the imperfections that persist no matter how much I grow.

You know how we do:

"I'm too this and not enough of that."

"I wish I had this and didn't have to deal with that."

"If only..."

The list goes on and on. Except, as I lay here in the bed, just me and God, and I hear him begin to speak (as he's been speaking all along), I only hear him say three words.

"I love you."

The words come to me, almost like a surprise gift. I inhale them like air that I've been gasping for and prepare for the tears that threaten to fall from my eyes.

That's what you've been trying to tell me? That's what I've been avoiding for so long? I lay in utter amazement.

"Yep, that's it.... I love you just as you are, and no matter how you feel, you are never alone."

I breathe a deep sigh of relief, happy that I finally stopped running. The tears I expected don't fall and instead I find myself smiling for no reason at all, as an intense feeling of peace covers me. For the first time I realize the meaning of "God's peace that surpasses all understanding."

After laying in the quiet for what seems like a wonderful bit of eternity, I finally respond, "I love you too."

Then, as almost an afterthought, as I turn over to find a comfortable position to reclaim my sleep, I add:

"I can't wait for our quiet time tomorrow."

What About Purpose?

Ten years. That's how long I've been espousing all of these grand ideas about how I'm going to leave my current job to find a profession that feels more purposeful for me. I've complained about it, vented about it, – heck, almost written a song about my dissatisfaction with not being where I'm "supposed to be." In fact, it's gotten so bad that my friends probably can already finish the conversation on my behalf. Being the good friends they are, they ride the waves with me. When I'm content with work – having made peace that for some reason I'm here, so I'll just suck it up – they listen patiently and never comment that I was saying something completely different the week before, and am likely to be singing a different tune the week after. Then, when I'm discontent, which is more the norm, they let me vent, never once asking why I've stayed in a place that makes me so unhappy and never once letting on they've heard it all before.

Maybe you've ridden the same waves in your profession? Maybe encountered those times when you knew deep in your spirit that God called you to do something . . . more? Maybe you don't even know what "it" is, but just have that indescribable inkling that there's something else out there? A certain need that God made you to fulfill?

There are moments when I have no doubt in my mind that my purpose-filled profession is waiting on me. That "thing" that will let me know why God placed me on this planet, and make me feel as if I've served some higher good. During those times, I slip into one of my grand daydreams of becoming the next Maya or Oprah or Tyler – or maybe, just the first imani. I grow excited at the possibilities.

Then a week, or month, or even a year passes. Then, doubt sets in. Despite my prayers and efforts, I find myself in the exact same place, without any sign that I've moved closer to this largely intangible goal.

Phase 1, I question whether I should be doing more to make it happen. Send out more letters or resumes? Talk with more mentors? Be more disciplined in my writing? Spend more time praying/meditating about exactly what it is I should be doing (because truth be told, I still don't fully know, which is yet another subject altogether).

Phase 2, I beat myself up for what I haven't done. If writing is part of my purpose, why has it taken me several years to write a book that other people might write in 6 months? Shouldn't it be easier? Why haven't I at least published articles or short stories? Why did I get comfortable going to work and coming home to start the cycle again, when I should have been on my hustle?

Phase 3, I question why I think I'm so special. Everyone else goes to work, does what they need to do and goes home to live. What makes me think I'm supposed to "live" on the job? And, what about gratitude? I mean, here I am with a good paying job that my ancestors – or, heck, my parents – would have been ecstatic to have. Isn't it a slap in the face to God when I ignore how blessed I am, and instead, keep asking for more?

Phase 4, I accept the fact that this is as good as it gets and consume myself with guilt work. In this period, I get in to work on time for a change and really grind, in honor of my daddy who had no choice but to work manual labor at a steel mill and in gratitude for being able to send money to help my mom who is ill.

If I'm lucky, I can stay in this last phase for months, all the while ignoring the little voice in the corner of my mind that still says "I want more."

Ten years. That's how long I've been doing this dance, and once again I've grown tired.

Except, this time is different.

At this moment, I KNOW that God has something more on the horizon for me because he has a purpose in mind that only I can fill.

At this moment, I KNOW that I won't miss it because he won't let me and I won't let me.

At this moment, I KNOW that it's coming soon, but I accept that 'soon' may not be measured in earthly time, so instead of counting the minutes, I need to make each minute count.

At this moment, I KNOW that it will happen at the perfect anointed time, which means this season of preparation is not only helpful, but necessary.

At this moment, I KNOW that where I am is exactly where I am supposed to be. I embrace this place, I make peace with this place, and I honor this place for all that it offers me and for all I can give right here and right now.

At this moment, I KNOW that I am already on purpose, even when it feels as though I'm not; and I am thankful for this.

God, I thank you for this moment that was not promised. Help me to live in it, embracing every single second of the gift that you didn't have to give. Give me peace in the "meantime," and help me not live as if I'm waiting for the "next time." Show me that your timing is always perfect. Remind me that all things are working for me, and I am exactly where I am supposed to be. Thank you for the vision for my future, even in its ambiguity. Let me be patient as you further define and refine it. When I question my purpose, as I undoubtedly will, remind me that the desires of my heart were placed there by you.

What About Loss?

Last year, I went to Aruba. Or, more accurately, I jetted off for a quick weekend getaway while my mother was in the hospital critically ill.

Does that sound callous? Selfish? Cowardly?

In hindsight, I must admit that it might have been all of the above. But, beyond those things, it was also necessary.

Have you ever faced the possibility of losing someone? Not just the thought of losing them one day, but the real likelihood of losing them at any given moment?

I hope you never know the pain of losing someone you love. It's one of those events in life that can't be described until you experience it firsthand. Even in the most spiritual person, who understands there is something better after this lifetime, there is a resistance to letting go. It's as if the mind can't quite wrap itself around the notion of not being able to hug them, see them, and hear their voice say "I'm here." Though the spirit knows all is well, the heart is often heavy.

That's what it felt like when I lost my father at the ripe old age of seventeen. I'd been with him when he died – seen what it looked like when he appeared to take his last breath and hold it. Saw the transition from a place of pain to the place of peace that knew no more suffering. I knew what it was like to celebrate the fact that he would hurt no more, and then to realize that it was a tradeoff because I hurt so much at the thought of him being gone. I remember like it was yesterday (instead of 19 years ago) how I walked around my college campus wondering how someone so special could disappear and life continue for the rest of the world. I can't lie, even now there are days when I still long for the things that only a daddy can do and say, and I miss him more than words can express.

That's why I literally freaked out as my mom unexpectedly went into the hospital last summer and had to have emergency stomach surgery. Although she'd suffered from Parkinson's Disease for several years, I hadn't truly processed the possibility of her leaving this earthly realm before me. That's why when I got the call that she had been hospitalized, I panicked. Once she was out of immediate danger, I ran.

I guess I could have gone home to stand over her bed "on watch," while I commiserated with my family. But, between her illness, the illness of another loved one, and a professional crisis that loomed, I was at emotional overload. I reasoned that if all I could do was wait and pray, why not wait and pray somewhere that would help me recharge and make peace with what might come? At the time, I felt as if I had no choice but to find a place where I could retreat – just me and God.

During my forty-eight hours in Aruba, I think I slept a total of 10 hours and spent the other thirty-eight in the beach water. From sun up to sunset, I was there, trying to wash away my fear, and if I'm honest, my anger. I talked to God, listened to God, pled with God, and finally accepted God in a way I had never done before.

I asked God how in the world I could ever make peace with the very real possibility of losing the woman who gave birth to me – whose very existence gave way to my own?

No, God didn't show me a burning bush as a sign. Nor did he part the seas as I swam. Nor did I hear his booming voice giving me the magical answer.

But he did give me peace.

As I looked out at the sun rising over the most beautiful water I'd ever seen, I noticed that no matter how I strained my eyes, I could not see where the ocean ended. In that single second, I was reminded that life is not finite. Just because we can't see a person after they transition, doesn't mean they're not there. Nothing ever really dies; it just changes shape or form. In the same way that I trust that God is there though he is not visible, so are our loved ones. They're always with us. In fact, sometimes when I close my eyes, and feel the wind blow, I feel my daddy's spirit blow through me and signify that all is well.

God also showed me my own selfishness in wanting to keep someone here in suffering, and caused me to unselfishly pray that my mother's days of pain never outnumber her days of peace, even if that means I have less time with her in the earthly realm.

But, mostly God gave me gratitude for having a mother for whom I could feel so much. One who taught me how to love and give and be who I am today. Who is by no means perfect, but who gave me a perfect foundation on which to build and grow. God taught me that a long-term illness shouldn't be seen as a curse, but instead, as a different kind of blessing. It's a reminder to keep our affairs in order and to live each day to the fullest. A reminder never to leave kind words unsaid, or to let pride make us unapologetic for the not so kind words that despite our best attempts, we sometimes utter. It's a cue to cherish each moment with those we love.

Amazingly, my mother recovered from her hospital stint and is now doing so much better. And, because of our scare last year, not a single day goes by without me thanking God for time that wasn't promised. I can't believe that I ever let months go by without saying "I love you," or let calls go to voicemail thinking that "there's always tomorrow."

Now I know that tomorrow isn't promised.

I'm not suggesting we carry on all the time as if we only have this moment, nor saying that we can't take anything for granted. . . .

Or, am I?

What About Faith?

I've heard it said a thousand plus times that "where there is fear, faith cannot exist." Each time I've heard it, I've assessed my own feelings and have come to the conclusion that I must not have any faith then!

It's not that I don't know God has got my back, and that ultimately, I will be ok. Somewhere WAY deep down in my spirit, I know this. It's just hard sometimes to tap into that part of myself when my current reality has some sticky situation I can't quite see myself through.

Have you ever known God was working it out, yet still felt terrified of the how and the when?

I've been down on my knees (literally) in my office at work praying that a professional situation would resolve itself – praying I was in fact perfect and hadn't committed any human error (because in my business human error can be known as malpractice). There have also been times when my stomach was in a gazillion cramping, burning, stabbing knots as I realized there was absolutely no way to meet all of the deadlines from the court and my clients.

I've made a really damaging error in my accounting (actually, it was more of an accountability error than an accounting one, because I just spent too doggone much), then felt my heart drop as I counted the number of days that remained until another check came in. For the wealthy and financially astute, you can just skip over this and read on, but I know there's at least one person who will feel what I'm talking about, even if you have to think back a ways – or even if you're too embarrassed to admit that you've been there.

I've sat in the car praying before going into the doctor's office to get test results, when it seemed that my brain literally could not compute what a negative report would mean for my future. I'm talking about calling up scriptures of Hezekiah's healing and "focusing on the positive" while I wondered if I was really strong enough to endure. Though I've never spoken in tongues, my prayers were so fierce that I really wouldn't have been surprised if something had just spewed out. I would have welcomed the opportunity to try anything to make sure God could hear me!

In fact, as I think back on it, there was a period of years when I can't remember NOT being scared. Heck, if I look in the medicine cabinet today, way back in the corner there's probably a package of tums/pepcid, just in case.

I know what folks mean when they say that faith and fear cannot co-exist, but I'm just not buying it because for me they've co-existed more often than not.

Faith got me off my knees in the office and helped me not stop in the midst of what felt like an impossible situation.

Faith made me think about how Jesus took a little and made it into a lot, and helped me prayerfully move forward although I couldn't really see how everything was going to get paid on time.

Faith helped me walk into that doctor's office, shaky legs and all, and face what could have been a life-changing report.

I was fearful alright! In fact, I was downright petrified! But, faith kept me moving forward, prayerfully believing that somehow, someway, I'd one day look back and tell the story of how I got over.

That's right; I did get over.

Because even in the midst of my fear, I recalled that there's never been a time when it didn't work out. Sometimes it worked out the way I'd hoped and prayed, and sometimes it worked out in a way that I couldn't have imagined.

But it always did.

Next time your heart is pounding a million miles per minute or your stomach has tightened into a nasty ball, tell yourself that it's ok to be afraid. After all, that's only human. Then stretch your mind back to the last time you felt that way. Remember how you couldn't physically see your way through – couldn't logically reason a way out – yet, somehow, someway, you still came out standing.

What About Confidence?

Have you ever wondered when Oprah Winfrey woke up and said "I'm really doing this! I AM a journalist! I AM a talk show host! I AM a producer! I AM an entrepreneur and philanthropist!"

I'm betting it was yesterday, and the day before that, and the day before that. . . .

You see, from talking with folks – from the most established to the person just getting started – I've found that most of us don't feel fully confident in what we are called to do until . . . well, actually never!

I was talking to a friend yesterday and his thoughts mirrored my own. He said "I keep waiting to be found out. I keep waiting for someone to discover that I'm not a *real* writer and that I've just been lucky so far." Now that statement makes perfect sense coming from me, because I have yet to publish a book, but from him it was just downright telling! He's the successful, published author of several books!

I wonder if the day will ever come when I can boldly and confidently say "I AM a writer." Or, even "I AM an attorney." Instead of feeling confident in what I do, I often feel as if I've just been fortunate enough to pull the wool over everyone's eyes so far. I was "lucky" enough to make it through law school and pass the bar the first time. Lucky enough to practice law for over a decade in very prominent positions. In the same way, I pray that luck and favor will get my books published before anyone realizes that I don't have a clue what I'm doing!

But, the funny thing is that NO ONE really knows what they're doing. Everyone is winging it. Everyone is praying that this project or that project turns out okay. Everyone has some insecurities about what they do and about what they want to do. We all begin with the question of "who am I to do ___?" We all start off feeling ill-prepared and unqualified, before we come to the realization: Why not me?

My point? We can be anything we want to be. No one is really prepared or qualified until they take the step of faith out and boldly proclaim "I AM a _____" even if at the time of proclamation, they don't have anything to show for it. That simple statement of intent gets the ball rolling and begins to make it into a reality.

What's the thing you've been holding back on because you don't feel properly qualified/prepared?

Do you honestly think you're any different from Oprah, when she hosted her first show? Tyler when he did his first play and movie? Maya when she wrote her first poem? Michael Dell when he quit school to pursue his business?

All of them started with a simple statement of "I AM," and kept moving forward until slowly but surely, it became true.

The only thing standing in between you and your dreams, is you.

Believe you can. And, in the meantime, do it anyway.

What About Obstacles To Your Purpose?

I've been doing this 5 a.m. writing thing for about 3 weeks now. Before that, it had been on my heart for about a month to get up in the mornings, but I just didn't think I could do it. After all, I LOVE sleep, and I was already struggling to get into my job at a decent time each day. How in the world would I fit in time to write?

But then a strange thing happened. I found myself unexplainably waking up a little before 5 without an alarm. That's when I simply couldn't deny the call anymore. That's when this little exercise began.

Slowly but surely, I began to embrace my new schedule, with the belief that after a few days my body would adjust and it would become natural. I even had grand visions of also running in the mornings, to increase my quiet time and to help me on the "Angela Bassett project" I've been threatening to complete for about a decade. My vision was so clear. I'd awaken without the alarm each morning, jump effortlessly to my home office and furiously write out whatever God placed on my heart. Once complete, I'd put on my workout clothes and run with ease like Gail Devers through my neighborhood. What a wonderful feeling of accomplishment I'd have each day!

Seeing as though they say it takes 21 days to form a habit, and seeing as though I know this desire to write is divinely inspired, I figured that once I got into the groove it would be easy. Right?

WRONG!

Of course, I absolutely love how it feels to look up 30 or 45 minutes after I've started writing and see that the page is full of thoughts I am excited to share – many of which I can't imagine coming up with on my own. It feels magical, and as compared to my first book – which was literally like a very long and painful childbirth – writing now feels so incredibly easy.

But, the entire process of writing, particularly in the mornings, still sucks!

If we're on purpose, aren't the stars supposed to just naturally align? Shouldn't we have the energy and discipline to make it so?

Let's just say that I'm still waiting for that magical moment. Instead of the way I envisioned it, this is the way it goes on most days:

It feels like I've just laid my head on the pillow and gotten into a comfortable groove. Then, bam! I'm disturbed by this noise that I can't quite identify. I finally realize it's my alarm clock, and to my dismay, see that it's already 5 a.m. Because I'm hardheaded about getting to bed early, this probably means that I've only slept about 4.5 hours.

I wrestle with God for another 30 minutes or so, half praying and half sleeping, while trying to figure out IF I'm going to get up. I can't lie. Some mornings I turn right over and go back to sleep. But on most days, the thought of doing what I'm called to do eventually, and tortuously, pulls me into a sitting position. Making it up and into my home office seems too arduous. Instead, I just pull the laptop into bed and manage to write without really getting up at all.

That usually goes somewhat smoothly – except that I quickly fall back to sleep after writing, and don't even attempt to run. I'm usually behind getting into the office. Let's not even talk about how tired I am by mid-day.

As if that isn't bad enough, there are days when I get up and wonder why it feels as if something is conspiring against me and making it even more difficult to fulfill my purpose.

Let's see, how about the day when while getting up I accidentally knocked over a vase on the nightstand and water dripped onto my keyboard? In addition to cleaning up the mess, it took me twice as long to type my thoughts because the letters were so sticky that I had to strike each one multiple times for them to work. . . . Or, what about the time when I went to bed early, but couldn't get to sleep until 3 a.m. so I only had two hours of sleep before the alarm went off! . . . Heck, what about today when my computer mysteriously has gone on the blink and I'm unable to use it at all?

Each time I meet with an obstacle, I want to climb back in the bed and give it up, at least for the day. I wonder why God hasn't made it easy for me, if this is a purpose he placed on my heart.

But there's this nagging desire inside of me that tells me not to give up. That desire keeps me going in spite of. Heck, that's why I'm typing today's thoughts on my blackberry. Talk about torture to write with your thumbs!

Maybe being on purpose doesn't mean it's always easy. In fact, maybe it means that sometimes more challenges may come your way to force you to determine if and how much you really want it. Maybe this book will be that much better because of the things I went through to birth it.

I don't know why when God calls us to do something he doesn't always clear the path in a way that makes for smooth sailing. But, I do know that whatever God has called you to do will come to fruition. Just believe and keep moving forward despite life's obstacles and difficulties.

Next time an obstacle comes your way and makes you question the purpose God has called you for, you tell it to move back, step aside, and shut it up, because this train is moving forward no matter!

What About Disappointment?

It's almost 6 a.m. and I just woke up. Unfortunately, the heaviness that threatened to weigh on me last night before I escaped to sleep has come down in full this morning. My heart wants to cry, but my mind reasons that I shouldn't be upset at all. Of course, my heart wins the battle hands down.

For what seems like an eternity, I've been in prayer for breakthroughs in each major area of my life. Professionally, I've prayed and thanked God in advance for securing me the right book deal, and moving me from my firm job into a purpose-filled profession. Physically, I've prayed for perfect health, the desire for only those things that will enhance my health, and the energy to get back on my workout program. Romantically, I've prayed for "him" while keeping my focus on "HIM" and being satisfied that I'm seeking the man that will complement (as opposed to complete) me, who will help me fulfill my purpose (and vice versa), and who can be my best friend and lover.

I've been praying and faithfully believing, and though many times it feels like I'm **so** close that I can almost reach out and touch it; at the end of the day, it appears as if I'm in much the same place as before.

My book has been miraculously moving into the hands of folks with influence, yet the offers I've received don't feel quite right to my spirit.

I feel so horrible about my job because it's a good job that many would kill for – yet, some days just being there threatens to suffocate me. And, last night I thought I'd make good networking connections at an event I strategically attended after scoping out the honorees only to find out that the honoree I wanted to meet opted for a concert (that I considered attending) instead! I spent good money on the event ticket, only to come home empty-handed.

As for my health, should I start with the fried food I've suddenly rediscovered or the intense sugar cravings that I've playfully called "Satan?"

But probably the biggest disappointment today is with love. Nah, I'm not walking around with my heart in my hand waiting to hand it off to the highest bidder. For all practical purposes, I'm doing well because I'm surrounded by so much love in every direction I turn. Still, if one more person tells me how sure they are that God is preparing someone SO special for me because I'm so ___, then I think I'll just scream! Of course I appreciate their words of encouragement and affirmation, and I relish their positive opinions of me, but some days it's like throwing gas on an open flame.

I guess I'm just tired. As I type, I'm wondering who in the world will even want to read this sad tale? Most days I've done well with taking myself out of the equation and writing after prayer, but maybe today I'm not in tune.

Is anyone else tired of being close, but not all the way there? Tired of waiting on the answer to your prayer, and tired of believing that it's going to be answered in due time?

God says there are people who feel exactly as I do, but who are afraid to say it. They fear they'll seem weak if they confess these types of feelings. Or, they think that admission would somehow undermine their faith. They're holding it in instead of speaking their truths at that moment, and asking God to renew their strength and optimism.

God says there are people who have lost their hope in having something "more" whether it's professionally, physically, romantically, or in some other area of their lives they have been praying on for some time.

I know I'm not the only one doing well for myself, but who occasionally, somewhere deep down, feels that I'm just flat out tired of being *close*, but not all the way "there."

So, what do we do?

First, we speak openly to God. Accept that it's okay to be disappointed, or even downright angry. It's ok. Besides, it's not like he doesn't already know our hearts.

If it's there, speak your truth and know that he'll understand.

Second, feel it. Just sit in your feelings for once instead of trying to magically wish them away without processing. I think we're so quick these days to move to the "I'm so good and so grateful" stage that we don't always give ourselves time to feel. Time to grieve the dream that hasn't yet come to fruition or a dream that we feel we've lost. We think we're being evolved by not feeling, but in actuality, we're suppressing emotions that will not be ignored. They'll come out when you least expect it. Sometimes as a blow-up, but more often (and distressingly), as a physical ailment.

Third – and this step only comes when you're completely done with number 2 – God said, "Pray again."

I asked, "Why? What's going to be different this time?"

God said, "You are."

I lay back in bed and take that in. I'm a little bit shocked that God hasn't grown tired of me asking him the same thing over and over. I wonder if his answer means that I'm never going to get my prayers answered and that I'll instead find myself at peace notwithstanding. But, I give it a try, and I begin to pray without any clue what I'll say.

God, I'm tired and I'm disappointed. Please renew me and restore my faith. Then, check the desires of my heart. Remove any that are not 'of you.' And, for those that remain, please at least give me some sign that I'm on the right path. Increase my patience. Enhance my peace and don't let me lose hope in the vision you placed in my heart.

The prayer gets me out of bed and lightens the load just a tad. As I drive into work, I feel it begin to take hold.

Soon after I get into the office, the phone rings. On the other end of the line is a classmate I haven't talked to in twelve years, with another potential connection for my book.

Thank you, God, for confirming that I'm on the right path. Thank you for your perfect time and your perfect peace.

Amen.

What About Joy?

I've often heard it said that "Joy is a choice." I must admit that I didn't really take it in the first few times, but tonight, as I prepare for bed, I find that this statement resonates with me, especially today.

I got up this morning with the weight of the world on my shoulders. Feeling like 'woe is me' because certain things in my life haven't taken off as quickly as I imagined. I could have gone to sleep in the same place in which I started, but instead I found myself making a different decision.

"Today, I choose joy."

This afternoon I talked to an old friend, who put things into perspective as he somewhat casually recounted the story of how he should have been killed in the 9/11 bombings. My friend worked in the World Trade Center for years before 9/11, and only survived the bombings because he decided to go in late that day. Both he and his assistant were amongst a small number of people from his company who survived, while SEVERAL HUNDRED of his friends and colleagues were killed.

He told me of how he arrived at the scene not long after the first plane hit, and watched the chaos firsthand. Of course, he mourned those who were lost, but he also gave thanks that his life was spared. This incident was a turning point in his life because it reaffirmed the value of the life we are given.

Kind of puts things in perspective, don't you think? I mean, here I am singing sad songs because I didn't make a business connect at an event, because I haven't YET moved into my dream profession, because I'm making bad choices about diet/exercise, and because I haven't YET met my dream man. But doesn't that miss the point?

Have you ever chosen to focus on what you don't have and what hasn't yet come to pass, instead of choosing to contemplate the things that should bring you joy each day?

I know that I'm only here by the grace of God and that I should be thankful because each day offers a plethora of new possibilities. That's why I can't afford to let a single day go by without saying "thank you."

Sometimes the gratitude list is filled with large miracles and blessings such as the one with my friend surviving 9/11, or maybe like the day when I see my first book in stores across the nation. But, on many days the gratitude list may seem insignificant, if you don't take a moment to relish it – appreciating each and every morsel.

Today, I am grateful:

- That I know what it feels like to love and be loved; because love is a gift. I'm grateful for God's boundless love, the love of my family and friends, and the past romantic love for which I have no regrets.

- To have a job that takes care of all of my needs and many of my wants; and a job where I have some autonomy and flexibility.

- For the homemade pizza that I made. It was not quite on the diet plan, but I enjoyed every bite!

- That all of my body parts are functioning such that I CAN choose to (or not to) exercise.

- For MANY leads in publishing, and for having finished writing a book that will change lives, whether it's two people or two million.

- For a warm Spring day full of sunshine.

- For a vision of more to come, and faith that it will.

I will not end this day in the way in which it started – that is, in a place of disappointment for things not yet seen. I understand I will have days when my load is heavy and my patience short; and I honor those feelings. But, negativity is a place that I choose not to stay. Right now I choose to release those feelings as I move toward the next day of miracles and possibilities.

Today, I choose joy. I urge you to do the same.

What About Discipline?

It's so easy to judge people with obvious addictions. The man on the corner begging for money to buy drugs. The woman in your office who can hardly wait for a break to run out and have a smoke. The extremely obese person who refuses to change their eating habits and exercise. They are all easy marks for our judgment. We look at them and think, "Why not stop already? You're killing yourselves!"

But, how many of us have as strong opinions when we look at ourselves in the mirrors?

Maybe it's consuming too much of things that are toxic to all of us, like caffeine, sugar, and alcohol. Or, maybe it's just continuing to eat after your body is full. Maybe it's the inability to start a workout program. Spending in excess, and living from check to check. Letting others walk over you; or conversely, responding in anger instead of in love. Speaking and thinking negative things about yourself and others. . . .

All of these things have the propensity to kill us. All of these are things we should strive to eliminate.

With that being said, who among us can cast the first stone?

Most days, if I 'graded' myself on performance in these areas, I'd find myself falling WAY short! In fact, if I was to chronicle in Bridget Jones fashion, my diary would look something like this:

- Salad and veggies consumed: 1 serving (not so good)
- Water consumed: 30 ounces (not so good)
- Flour and sugar consumed: as much as I wanted (not so good)
- Exercise: many, many reps of fork to mouth (not so good)
- Negative thoughts about my job: 3,946,000 (not so good)
- Negative thoughts about certain co-worker(s): 5,456,789 (better than yesterday)

That's on a good day!

Changing habits isn't always easy. Because none of us is perfect, letting go of bad habits is a never-ending journey. But, with prayer and discipline, it can become a reality.

Although we aren't all labeled as addicts in the literal sense, I think we can all benefit from the addicts' creed of "one day at a time."

Whatever it is that you're struggling with, don't try to wrap your brain around your ultimate goal. Saying I want to become Angela Bassett fine when you're currently packing Nell Carter pounds, might just be a bit much for you to take in at one time. Instead, each day wake up with the proclamation:

"Just for today, I will do better."

Use that mantra for every area of your life. Eating better. Exercising more. Being a better steward of your money and time. Being a better employee or business owner. Keeping your peace. Staying grounded in a more positive place. Acting in love.

Don't overwhelm yourself with notions of what might happen tomorrow. Instead, make a decision to do better just for today.

When you fall off the wagon, as you (and I) inevitably will, don't be too hard on yourself. Chances are you feel guilty enough already. Instead, lovingly ask yourself how you can do better. Then choose to do so the next day.

And, the next day. And, the next . . . .

What About Ego?

It's funny. When I first started writing these inspirational, rambling nuggets, I had no idea how they'd benefit me or anyone else. Then, when I began to share these thoughts, and envisioned the possibility of even publishing them one day, I became extremely excited about these wonderfully 'sexy' topics that I could opine on to help someone else along the way. The funny thing is, the more I write from the spirit – that is, removing my own self and ego from the equation, the more my writings take on a direction of their own. More often than not, the writings aren't extremely glamorous, and they touch (sometimes painfully) on areas in my own life where I need to grow.

Today, **I** wanted to write about some hot topic that **I** thought might make for stimulating discussion. **I** had a ton of ideas, and **I** was well on my way to some creative masterpiece until **I** stopped and took "**I**" out of the equation. It's as if God was telling me, "Enough about you, already!"

Then he probably paused dramatically, winked and said, "Then again, if you want this to be about you, then so be it!"

God didn't have to say anymore. Instead, after setting the stage, he allowed me to take stock of how many times I've started a thought or deed with the word "I."

As my mind flashed back through my quiet time with God, the morning writing, and even my recent impatience with certain things in my life; I realized that I'd be a whole lot better off if I was less self-centered.

Had I really prayed about God moving me to my purpose-filled career with pure and unselfish motives? Did I ever make the move about doing work that he needed and helping those that he placed in my path? Or, was it just about my own disdain with corporate America? And, yes, I'll admit it, my own, selfish desire to be on Oprah?

Had I really prayed about being the helpmate for a man who has a similar purpose to fulfill – about complementing him and supporting him in his quest to do all that God called him to do? Or, was it just about me wanting "my King" for my own benefit?

Had I really prayed to be a better steward of my finances so that I could help others in need, and help others pursue their path? Or, was it more about me getting paid, so that I could live comfortably (which includes, of course, having tons of shoes and handbags)?

On days when I felt discontent that nothing magical seemed to happen, did I take it as an opportunity to create magic for someone else?

What about you? How often do your prayers start and end with the word "I"?

Suddenly, I realized that maybe my entire paradigm was wrong.

I'm not suggesting that we shouldn't want the creature comforts – from a man, to a mad bank account, to a job I like – because we want to enjoy them. It's not like unselfish motives weren't already *part* of my agenda. I'm just suggesting that maybe we need to check ourselves, and keep rechecking ourselves periodically, to ensure that selfish gain is never the primary motivation for anything we do.

Maybe if we take ourselves more out of the equation and focus on someone else, or on our collective greater good, maybe this whacky thing we call life will make more sense.

Why don't we try an experiment? I'm willing to try if you are!

The next time you're having a bad day – I'm talking one of those days when you just want to roll over and go back to bed, but you realize that taking any more sick days will likely cause you to be labeled as deathly ill by your boss, so you have to go in and suck it up – Well, the next time you have one of those icky days, stop and pray about how you can bless someone else. That's right. Take the focus off of whatever it is in your life that seems so pressing and flip the switch to a loved one or stranger in need.

Can you imagine if you called one of your friends who has been running crazy or having a hard time and said "I know you've been stressed. Can I treat you to dinner tonight?" Doesn't matter if it's something grand, like sending flowers, a card, or even a financial blessing unexpectedly given to a friend, or something "small," like calling just to say "I love you." I guarantee that if you're prayerful about who you choose and what to send, God will let you be an angel to someone else who's having an even worse day and will allow you to bless them right where they need it. You know what else? Not only will it give them the magic they needed to make it through the day; you might just find a little residual magic rubs off on you!

For the single women, next time you're feeling discontent that your King hasn't yet arrived to rescue you from this madness they call dating, focus on some area in your life that you can grow in so that you'll be a better mate once he arrives. I tell you, the only thing worse than the thought of my Prince not coming, is the thought of God sending him my way, then him running off because my stuff is not together. Scary!

Now, just in case the married women feel as if they're getting off easy, let me suggest that it doesn't stop after the wedding! In fact, that's when it begins. Next time you're feeling as if your husband hasn't listened enough, hasn't supported you enough, isn't complementing you in the way that you want; take the focus off self and show him by example.

There it is. Not sexy or glamorous, and surely not even what **I** wanted to talk about this morning.

But, then again, maybe it's not about me.

What About Agape Love?

When I was little, and I made my mother mad, there were times when I thought she might maim or disown me. In fact, I can still vividly hear her casually saying things like:

"If you ever got strung out on drugs, I'd just have to put you out and change the locks on the door."

Yep, and she said it with such cool finesse that I almost wondered if I'd heard her right!

Or, what about my all time favorite, fall-back threat when I was little and did something really bad? My mother – who was not a violent woman to speak of – would look me square between the eyes and say:

"Don't you know that I will knock fire out of you?"

I don't know how old I was before the fear of fire actually spewing from some part of my body diminished, and I was able to hear what she was really saying, which I think was, "Don't test me!"

But, strangely enough, no matter what my mother threatened me with, or how painful it sounded, I knew deep down in my spirit that she would never, ever stop loving me. Didn't matter if I was on drugs, pregnant, and flunked out of school. Didn't matter if I killed somebody, her love was and is forever. Now, she might not have come to see me in jail, but I knew that she'd always love me and be praying for me, because I was a part of her. Flesh of her flesh; bone of her bone.

When I think back on it, this has to be my greatest earthly example of agape love. Who else in my life has loved me with unconditional abandon; without thought of reciprocity or gain?

Or, as importantly, who else have I loved in this way?

Agape love teaches us that when you love someone – really, truly love someone in the way that God loves us, it never ends.

Have you ever loved someone without any thought of reciprocity? Even when by your standards they didn't deserve it?

I'd like to say that I have, but the truth is, I'm not sure. I thought about past relationships and friends that I no longer have in my life. I let my mind reflect on people who have done some really foul things to me, and who I'd just as soon not ever see again. I remembered people who I'm sure in hindsight 'loved' me because it was convenient or because of what I gave, without understanding who I am.

God, are you saying that I'm supposed to love EVERYONE in the agape way?

As soon as the question was out of my mouth, I realized the answer. It's as if God replied and said, "Why not? That's how I love EVERYONE . . . including you!"

No, I'm not suggesting that the battered wife has to stay in a marriage till death do her part. Nor am I endorsing a relationship where anyone is being disrespected, used, or forced to settle for less than what God has for them.

Believe you me, I've done my own misinformed version of agape love – the kind that had me trying to love enough for the both of us. No, there is definitely a time to let go of people who are unable or unwilling to reciprocate the love and respect we give freely.

But, what I am suggesting is that even if that person can't sit in the "front row" of your life anymore –even if they can't even sit in the theater – you should still learn to love them right where they are.

Why? Because we should all try to be that great personification of love. Why else? Because carrying around anything other than love is more of a detriment to you than to them. That hatred, or non-love, eats away at the very things that are good inside of you and diminishes your peace, your spirit, and possibly, your health.

Instead of hate or non-love or conditional love, try loving them (even if it's from afar) in their imperfections and brokenness; insecurities and anger; manipulations and control dramas . . . .

Try to love them, just as God loves you.

What About The Illusion Of Control?

Each morning I wake up, log onto the computer, and then sit anxiously wondering about the topic of the day. No matter how many days I do this, it always begins with the same five minutes of utter panic. I worry I won't know what to write about, or that the right words won't come to mind. I question whether what I've written before is any good, whether my thoughts will touch anyone, and whether anyone will ever get to read them.

My mind moves at warp speed through a host of potential subjects that make sense, but don't feel right to my spirit. My heart begins to race faster, and my mind says things like, "Well, it had to happen sooner or later. This is the end of the road on the little writing thing you wanted to try." On a really bad day, I hear things like, "Did you really think that *you* could write a book? Ha!"

Knowing that the little demons in my mind are just getting started with their attack on my confidence, and it's now or never on shutting them down, I take a deep breath, close my eyes, and begin to pray.

"God, what would you have me to write today?"

As I breathe in and out deeply, I begin to feel the muscles in my body relax, and an eerie calmness takes over. In a matter of minutes, my mind slows and eventually quiets in full. Only when I find this peaceful place am I able to stop thinking, and *feel* what I should write.

First, a question comes to mind, then a first sentence; and, then the next. Unlike my usual writing, I don't try to figure out where I'm going next. I don't censor or edit. I don't even think. I just let the spirit lead me wherever it will, trusting intuitively that though I don't know the end destination, I'll end up in the right place at the right time.

Miraculously, there hasn't been a time when I didn't get there. There also hasn't been a time when I could look back and understand how I arrived. I only know that thirty or forty minutes later, I make it home. As I type the last sentences of my inspirational nugget, I feel such a peace in knowing that I did.

Can you imagine what it would be like to function like this in every area of your life?

This morning I find myself wishing I could. Admit that I don't know where I'm going, where I'll end up, and if I'll get there at the right time. Instead of trying to maintain this illusion of control – instead of trying to figure it all out with my mind – stop, close my eyes, breathe in and out deeply until I find my peace, then listen to my spirit as it leads me step by step to where I need to be.

Can you imagine doing that in everyday life? I can. I can also imagine me stopping every few steps to question, "Where am I now? Where am I going next? When will I get there? What's the ultimate destination? Just tell me already because this blind following is a bit much!" Instead of just trusting, and knowing, and letting my spirit guide me to exactly where I need to be.

It's not easy to walk in the dark without a clear destination. But, I realize that when I've been able to do this – even for short spurts in my life – it's at those times when I've opened my eyes to find myself someplace more beautiful and extraordinary than I could have ever navigated on my own.

The next time I find myself sitting in life with all those questions racing through my mind about where I am, where I'm going, and when I'm going to get there; I'm just going to stop right in that place. I'm going to close my eyes, take a deep breath, and begin to pray.

"God, what would you have me to do?" Then, I'll take one step forward. And, then the next . . . .

What About Being In The Moment?

I used to love the saying that "life is a journey, not a destination." It sounded all snazzy and cute to spout off at the right time. It also conjured up images of me sitting in a yoga position, sipping tea, and feeling all "Zen."

It was real cute and all, except on those days when it felt like the monkey was on my back. When I wanted to scream "please let something happen already!" as I sat in my corporate office, trying to look appropriately engaged, while being bored to tears with what I was doing.

Yeah, I was all about the journey, until it took me several years to write a book, and until I was faced with the horrible circumstances that gave rise to that book. I mean, when you're going through a major life crisis, it's really hard to "be in the now" and be happy about it, when all you really want to do is get to the next minute, hour, day, month, and year – in hopes that when you get there, it will be a place less painful than the one you're currently in.

No matter how balanced we are, I think it's human nature to long for the next thing and the next thing and the next thing. But it's a temptation we have to resist.

Do you know how many big moments we've likely missed because we were already daydreaming about the next one?

It's like the woman who longs to get married. She spends her days and nights fantasizing about this great guy who's going to sweep her off her feet. Years go by, with romantic and platonic friends coming into her life to teach her things that will help prepare her for her King, but she's too busy looking for "the one" to spend time learning the lessons. It takes a minute for him to arrive. But, finally he does.

He's enjoying her company. He's enjoying each moment that they spend growing together. She's dreaming about the proposal.

He finally pops the question. She is ecstatic . . . for about an hour. She's on top of the world. But then, she starts dreaming about the wedding.

He's enjoying the engagement, enjoying spending time with her and growing with her. But she's so busy reading wedding magazines and planning the wedding; the engagement is almost a blur.

At last, the big day arrives! She is ecstatic . . . for about a day. She's on top of the world. But, then she starts dreaming about children. . . . And so on, and so on. . . .

Fast forward a few more dreams and she's dead.

Okay, I know there's lots of exaggeration in my little story, but you must admit that the basis of it is true! Most of us spend so much time waiting on the next thing, that we miss the beautiful thing happening right at that moment.

Every day, we miss little miracles. As we rush off to work, we don't take note of God smiling at us through the sun, or of God giving us a hug through the wind and rain. We don't hear him in the music we play, or taste him in some scrumptious meal.

Instead, most often, we don't enjoy the moments at all. It's like we've fast-forwarded through the bridge of a song, without realizing that the bridge is sometimes the very best part.

God, as tempting as it is for me to rush through my life to the next Big thing, help remind me that every day I'm able to breathe, and laugh, and love – all of these days are filled with Big things. Help me to be in the moment and to express gratitude for each one that wasn't promised. Help me to cherish the journey.

What About The Cocoon?

Earlier this week, I shared with a friend my inspirational nugget about change – about the caterpillar who doesn't want to become a butterfly. Her response was "Girl, I feel where you're coming from. But what about those of us who really want to become butterflies, but just want to skip past the cocoon stage?"

I laughed when she asked that, but then I realized that it was a really good question.

Have you ever realized that the cocoon is necessary, but still needed something to hold onto while going through?

In or about June 2000, I had a strong desire to write a book. The only problem was that I didn't even know where to start. Nor did I know what I should write about. I'd always loved writing, and I majored in journalism in undergrad, but writing a book placed me in unfamiliar territory. I'd never even written a short story!

I kept thinking about it and praying about it. Finally one night I decided to pray before I went to sleep, and to ask God to speak to me in my dreams. Though he'd never done so before, I thought just maybe I could hear better with less interference.

I still vividly remember the dream I had that night. In it, I was talking to someone else, but instead of speaking normally, we read our "lines" from pieces of paper that we held.

When I woke up, I didn't understand. Then suddenly, I realized that God was telling me that my life is a script!

I excitedly journaled my response from God, and I was all animated until I realized there was one major problem: absolutely nothing had happened in my life worth writing about. Sure, I'd gone through a few things here and there, but for the most part, I'd had very few challenges that might interest anyone else.

The next month, my sister (who is a minister) was visiting me and my then husband. While she was with us, she prophesied that my husband would come to a place of brokenness, that through this experience I would come to know my true strength, and that our marriage would become a ministry for others.

We heard her say these words, but didn't know what to do with them because things were good for us. We thought that maybe her words had to do with my husband's business not taking off as quickly as we'd hoped, or something along those lines. But, we never expected what was to come.

Several weeks later the rug was pulled out from under me as I found myself driving my husband of five years to a mental hospital, and learned that he'd been unfaithful with numerous women throughout our marriage. To say I was hurt would be a serious understatement. I didn't know I was capable of producing that many tears, or that a heart could literally feel as if it was broken.

Yet, as I went through the next several months, with things getting much worse before they got even a little bit better, there was a small voice in the corner of my mind that kept telling me "Remember, I told you that your life is a script, and from this you'll have something to share with the world. This was all ordained."

Now, I'm not saying the thought of writing a book made me feel all warm and fuzzy, or took away the hurt I was feeling. Nor did the prophecy about me being stronger and having a marriage ministry make me feel good. But, I did take some small comfort in knowing that God told me in advance that this hurtful phase of my life was something I was going to go "THROUGH." This was my cocoon.

Today, as I reflect on my friend's words, I find myself asking, is it easier to get through the metamorphosis if we know we'll come out better on the other side? If we know that our lives may be a testimony for someone else? That is, did the prophesy and dream give me something to hold onto in the meantime?

But, wait a minute. I know my story is a bit unique in that I had a dream and received a direct word, but even without them, shouldn't we always know that we're going to emerge better on the other side? Even if not through a dream or word, hasn't God already promised us that we ALWAYS come through our valleys stronger, better, and wiser than before?

All of our lives are scripts in the sense that our challenges should be shared with others. Only by sharing, can we help someone else as they are going through. All of us have been given the same word from God that broken times will come and afterwards we will be stronger for it.

All of us have something to hold onto.

If you're going through something today, hold on and know that God has said this place you're in is temporary and you will come out on the other side infinitely better than you could ever imagine.

If you've already emerged from your cocoon – or even if you're still in the midst of it, seize the opportunity to share your experiences with someone else. I guarantee there will be healing in this, not only for the person you share with, but also for you.

What About Me?

Let me paint the scene. You're sitting in your office in the middle of what has become your "normal" weekly breakdown. You're torn between acting like everything is okay, and just literally picking up your bag and walking to your car without even one backward glance. Your attempt to smile at a co-worker looks more like a grimace, and you realize that everyone – even the receptionist – knows that you are praying that God miraculously delivers you from this position right here and right now.

Your phone rings, and it's your best friend on the other end. Hoping for some good news to get you through this anxious moment, you listen intently as she says:

"Oh my God, I've got great news!"

You smile, and hold your breath, as she pauses dramatically.

"I just got a call about a job. It sounds like it was made for me! I can't believe it!"

Your smile freezes in mid-stride, but you don't know why, as you congratulate your friend – your dear sister-friend – on the call that could greatly change her circumstances. You say all of the right things, express all of your heartfelt happy sentiments, and truly mean every single word. But, somewhere in the corner of your mind, if you dust off the cobwebs and search for what's underneath, there's a small, shy (and somewhat guilty) voice asking:

"But, what about me?"

Maybe you're not as self-centered as I am, and being the Saint that you are, those types of thoughts have never entered your mind. But, me? I have to admit, though it has been brief, that little envious monster has tried to creep into my space numerous times in even the past several days.

On Thursday, it was the call from a friend who said "Girl, guess what? I'm engaged! He asked me to marry him!"

Then, on Monday, it was the call from a friend who said "Girl, guess what? I'm pregnant! We're having a baby!"

Finally, on yesterday, it was the call from a friend who said "Girl, guess what? I just got a call about a job! It sounds like it was made for me!"

Now, being the person I am, I thought it was pretty good that my pity party didn't start until last night, when all of these calls merged into one in my mind. When my little mysterious funk could no longer be dismissed as normal monthly moodiness, I had to start taking inventory of what in the world was going on and face the fact that I was experiencing a much unwanted bout of envy.

Envy is a word I never, ever thought I'd use to describe my emotions. I was successful in my own right, loved my friends, and took joy in celebrating their blessings as my own. Then, why had the green-eyed (or whatever color its eyes are) monster, chosen me? Why had I let it choose me? Was I some horrible person for having these thoughts?

Have you ever felt like God was sharing blessings with everyone else, and it was taking a wee bit too long for your turn?

This morning, as I got up, I was determined to figure it out so that I could go from funky to fun on this wonderful Wednesday morning. A full week of restless feelings and interrupted peace was about all I could take. I wanted my peace back!

When I prayed, I realized that envy is one of our worst enemies. It's one of the many tricks our mind plays on us to keep us distracted and to interrupt our peace. It's just like gossip, or any other negative thought – it's a mindset that will feed upon itself, and grow, if we allow it.

The little "gremlin" (as one of my friends calls it) says things like, "Why is *she* getting married and not you? You've been single longer than her!" Oh yeah, that gremlin voice can get so ugly that it says things I can't even dare repeat!

That negative spirit doesn't want you to understand that because we are all God's children, each time he blesses one of us, it's a blessing for all of us.

The same negativity doesn't want you to remember all the things your friend went through to get where she is – things you wouldn't haven't wanted to experience and some things you probably don't even know.

It doesn't want you to realize that your path is uniquely your own, and **what God has for you is just for you** – such that you wouldn't want to change places with your friend. Think of it this way, "Would you want to be marrying the guy your friend got engaged to? Working at the job she told you about? Having a baby at this very moment under your present circumstances?" I don't know about your response, but mine was "He—e–ck (oops, almost slipped), NO!"

Don't fall for the okie doke and trick yourself into losing peace because your friend – someone you love and want nothing but happiness for – is being blessed! It ain't got nothing to do with you, except that it's God showing you how he's moving and that he's got everything under control if you just sit your little behind down and wait your turn.

Father God, thank you for showing me the good, the bad, and the downright ugly within my heart. Now that you've shown it to me, I ask you to remove it and anything else that comes from the spirit of envy. I know envy is not of you, because it's the opposite of love, and I know I don't want it to be part of me. Right now, I release it, squash it, drop kick it, and bury it somewhere so deep it cannot rise up again. I thank you for my friend's blessing, and I celebrate it as if it was my own. . . . I know you haven't forgotten about me, but instead, you're preparing the blessing that is just for me at the perfect anointed time. Amen.

What About Progress?

I'm beginning to think I have some sort of weird fascination with caterpillars. It's not just that this is the third time I've been inspired to write about them; it's that now I've taken to actually seeing them!

This weekend I went running on a high school track not far from my house. I was running at what I considered to be my Flo Jo/Gail Devers speed, but in reality, a little old lady with a cane could probably have strutted past me. In any event, I was still feeling pretty good about myself because after taking quite a long break from my workout routine, I was finally back on track.

As is usually the case, when I got to about the third or fourth lap around the track, I started praying. Not in an organized and traditional way. Instead, I was just praying for strength to keep running. I can only imagine how crazy I looked sometimes as I completed a lap and waved my hand up in the air like I was sitting on the second pew of church, giving thanks for a really good word.

On this particular day, I was just praying for God to send me some strength, and talking bad about myself for not running more often.

Then, the funniest thing happened. I looked down by my feet and a stone's throw away was a real, live caterpillar. Unlike the one I described in my early writings, this one was actually kind of cute. She was a black and gold, furry little creature in the most inner lane of the track, appearing to try to make her way across the lanes to the outer lane and beyond to the grass.

I smiled to myself, then quickly refocused on the task at hand. Careful not to step on the caterpillar, I began praying again and turned up my music so that I could keep moving, despite my fatigue.

I almost forgot about the caterpillar, until I got to the same place on the track on my next lap. As I came to that place, I began to look on the ground so that I could make sure not to step on it.

I looked across the second and third lanes of the track and saw nothing. I began to think that it had already made it to its destination.

Finally, just as I was coming up on the last curve, I looked down right in front of me. There, seemingly in the same spot as it was before, was my caterpillar. It was still moving across that same interior lane, and probably was only a few centimeters from where I'd seen it the first time.

My first thought? God, it must really suck to be a caterpillar!

My second thought – a bit more centered – was a question. I found myself wondering, when the caterpillar is moving that slowly, can she even tell that she's making progress? Heck, I almost couldn't tell because she was moving so slow. But, checking my surroundings again, I confirmed that she was definitely in a different place than the first time I saw her.

That caterpillar became my ultimate motivator as I ran my miles that day. Each time I circled the last corner for another lap, I looked and saw that the caterpillar had moved a bit closer to its goal. And, so did I.

Of course, my energy increased as I realized that God showed me the caterpillar as a representation of myself. After all, what are the odds of noticing a tiny caterpillar on a track? I haven't seen a caterpillar in years, and certainly not while running!

But, this one – this teeny, little insect – was meant to show me a valuable lesson.

For the past several weeks, I've been singing the blues about how nothing in my life is moving. Writing about the purpose I fear that I have yet to fulfill, and the dreams that still seem so far out of grasp.

In a nutshell, I've felt as if I'm no closer to my goals than I was last month or even last year, and I've questioned whether I'll ever get there.

But, the caterpillar reminded me that sometimes it's hard to see our own progress. In fact, I'm betting the caterpillar probably didn't feel like she was moving either . . . until she reached the other grassy side and finally could look back to where she started.

Sometimes we're so busy looking at how far we have left until we reach our goals, we don't realize how far we've already come.

Have you ever felt as if you're just treading water instead of moving steadily towards your goals?

The next time you're feeling as if any part of your life is stagnant – as if your goals are still far outside your reach – take a moment to reflect. Look back to months and years past at where you were and take inventory. If it's still not clear, call a friend for their perspective because sometimes it's easier to see from the outside. Have them remind you of where you were five years ago so that you can really appreciate your journey.

Next, pat yourself on the back for the progress you've made. Start with any physical/tangible progress, but then don't forget about the mental, emotional, and spiritual strides as you've changed your thinking, learned your lessons, and grown.

Finally, as you move toward your future, set some short term goals so that you can achieve gratification while on the way to your goals and dreams. Maybe you won't make it all the way across the track in a day or week or even a year, but perhaps you'll make it to the next lane. That's progress and cause for celebration!

Dear God, today I know I'm not yet where I want to be, but right now I thank you that I'm not where I used to be.

What About Obedience?

Sometimes I have this image of God sitting up watching scenes from my life in the same way that I might watch an episode of "Grey's Anatomy" or in the way that I might watch a basketball game on TV. I see him with a huge tub of popcorn, nearly bowled over in laughter at some of the things I do. At other times, I see him walking up within touching distance of the "screen" and screaming: "No, no, no! What are you doing? Don't you know you're gonna . . . . Ooops, well, I guess you wanted to find out the hard way!"

Haven't you ever known in your spirit that you should do things a certain way, but you instead decided to strike out on your own?

Maybe this doesn't ring a bell for you, but God and I go through this little exercise almost daily. As I'm going about my normal activities, I'll begin to do something. It could be as simple as picking up the phone to make a call that I know I should be prayerful about, and I'll feel God move to the edge of the couch and say, "I really don't think you should make that call now. Maybe later after you've calmed down."

But, I stubbornly walk over and pick up the phone.

God stands up and says, "Aw, man, I'm telling you, I don't think you should do it."

I start dialing the number anyway.

Then God walks right up on me, so close that I can feel him next to me, and he says, "This is not going to be good. Just stop now!"

I press talk on my phone.

God sits back down, covers his eyes and thinks, "Man, I don't even want to see how this turns out!"

Okay, so maybe it's a bit extreme for me to compare God to a movie/TV/sports watcher. Maybe a better analogy is of an all knowing parent who tells their child not to do something, then sits and calmly watches as he/she decides to go against what they've been told. I'm sure if you stretch your mind way back, you can remember something really crazy you did as a child, just because you wanted to find out for yourself if fire was really hot, or what happens if you put a fork into an electric socket, or exactly why you shouldn't play hide and seek in the dark.

No matter how many times your mother or father told you not to do x or y or z, you had to try it for yourself. It was almost as if it was calling to you, saying, "Hey, nothing's going to happen! Just give me a try!"

That's why you were completely shocked and amazed when you burned your hand, got your first electric shock, or broke something (in the house or on your body) as you ran around in the dark. In fact, you almost had the nerve to say or think something like, "Aw, man! Why did this happen to me? I was just minding my own business!"

While I try not to live my life with regrets, or with notions of what *might* have happened if I'd chosen a different path, every now and again I allow myself to reminisce so that I can learn from my past. I think back on the times when I KNEW in my spirit that I shouldn't go to a certain place or do a certain thing. Or, on the flip side, I think back on times when I KNEW in my heart there was something I should do: when I should apologize to someone, forgive someone for what they did, forgive a debt that God told me to let go of, be more disciplined in some area of my life so that I would be prepared when another opportunity came along . . . . The list goes on and on. But, many times I didn't listen and instead was righteously indignant when things turned out differently than I imagined. Only later, when I rewound the events in my mind, did I remember that I should have known better.

As I shake my head in recollection, I can't help but to smile as I realize the beauty of God is that he doesn't keep track of all the times when we don't listen. He never says I told you so. In fact, he takes those same "mis-steps" and uses them for our good. If we prayerfully move forward, what could have been labeled as a mistake, actually can turn into our greatest blessing.

Today, take a moment to think about the things in your past you've learned from and how they've shaped who you are today. Instead of feeling guilt or regrets, experience gratitude for each one. And, when you're done, commit to taking more time to listen and follow that inner voice that never steers us wrong.

What About Our Thoughts?

I remember when I found out that one of my favorite aunts was diagnosed with Parkinson's Disease. I was devastated. I couldn't imagine how someone who was so full of life could possibly become an invalid.

Every time I went home to Houston, I watched for signs the disease was progressing. Sure enough I noticed a few changes in my aunt as the years went on. She moved slower, sometimes had tremors, and was often less steady. But, two things never changed: she always wore a smile that could light up a room, and she was always full of a zest for life. It didn't matter if she got out of the car walking a little sideways, my aunt continued to drive, live fairly independently, and even played the piano on many occasions, for many, many years.

Once someone overheard my aunt's prayers, and heard her say these words:

"God, thank you that I have my health and strength. Please, Lord, bless those less fortunate than me, who aren't well."

Here was a woman who by society's standards was seriously ill, yet, she called herself "healthy" and lived a healthy life. How could someone with a "debilitating illness" be thankful for their health? How could she be so incredibly happy?

I realize now that my aunt knew a secret to life that many of us never, ever learn: Our thoughts and words are the most powerful tools we have. In biblical terms, there's power of life and death in the tongue. Philippians also encourages good thoughts by saying when we think on good things, the peace of God is with us.

Haven't you ever noticed that what you focus on often becomes your reality?

Don't believe me?

Just ask a doctor about some of their "miracle" cases and they will show you that a patient with a positive attitude is far more likely to heal than the one who takes on the illness as their identity, and envisions the worst fate.

Or, ask my girlfriend who was given the worst possible prognosis early in her pregnancy, yet against the odds, delivered a fully healthy baby girl, with no complications.

Heck, ask me about how I struggled to write a book for YEARS, but only finished it when I stopped doubting myself, began to call myself an author, and believed that it could be done.

On the other hand, how many times have you declared it to be a "horrible day" only to find that your words were a self-fulfilled prophecy? Or, talked negatively about your work situation, then found the environment became even more hostile? Or, worried yourself to death about a health situation, then wondered why it continued to worsen?

No doubt, there are things in this world outside of our control. But, we do control our thoughts and words. If we make them thoughts and words that give life, promote healing, personify positivity and love – we have that much more chance of living lives that exhibit the same.

My aunt lived a life that was longer and healthier than most people I know, all because she knew one of the secrets to life.

Now you know it too.

What About Hope?

Whether you're an old or new friend, you've undoubtedly heard me talk about my desire to be on the Oprah Winfrey show, right? I've joked about it, prayed about it, visualized it, and thanked God in advance for putting the right people in my path. Never mind that I'm probably one of a zillion folks who share this same dream. I decided to believe.

Several days ago, I met up with a couple of my classmates from law school. As we caught up on recent events, one of them asked how he could help with my goal of becoming a published author. I was shocked at the question because here was someone I hadn't seen in years offering to help me, without asking for anything in return.

Unfortunately, I'm horrible at asking for assistance, so though he opened the door, I kind of danced around the topic of whether he knew any publishers or editors. When he didn't, I swallowed my fleeting disappointment and continued talking about other things.

The conversation went on, and I put aside any notions of a good networking connection until sometime later in the discussion, when a chance comment changed everything.

As I've often done before, I made a joke about being on Oprah. My friend paused, appeared to reflect momentarily, and then calmly said:

"I can get you to Oprah."

Of course, my heart stopped as I tried to figure out if I'd heard him right and if I understood him correctly. I remained silent as he continued to tell me that he knows one of Oprah's producers, and she's always looking for good stories.

Yes, after a few years of joking about it, praying about it, visualizing it, and thanking God for it; I finally have an opportunity to submit my story to one of Oprah's producers. I'm extremely excited about the possibility of being on Oprah's show; but I must admit that in this moment, I'm more in awe of God at putting the right folks in my path. I mean, how many folks know one of Oprah's producers?

I used to be the type to hold my dreams somewhat close to the vest until I believed it to be a sure thing. I told myself the disappointment would be greater if it didn't work out and I had to share bad news with the masses. But, in reality, I think I was afraid to hope. That's why my sharing this with you is a testimony to how far I've come, and also an example of how we should live, without fear of hoping and with gratitude for how God has already worked it out. True enough, it doesn't always work out in the way we envisioned; but it always comes together.

People always ask me how certain things happen to/for me. If I want to meet someone or want to do a certain thing, lots of little miracles typically align to make it so. I've even had my friends jokingly say that I must have an inside line to God. But, in reality, things happen to/for me because I "speak them" everywhere I go. I tell the cab driver and the doorman and the waiter and people I meet in passing about my dreams. Why? Because each time I speak it, I reaffirm my faith in it and show God that I believe him to be true. Each time I speak it, I invite others to participate in helping me reach my dreams. I'm telling you, it works! This is how I've gotten EVERY job since law school, as well as how I've gotten countless other "chance" meetings/events. This is how I came to be on a Tyler Perry set for the filming of his new movie a few weeks back. And, I won't even mention the time a security guard said, "You want to meet Prince? Okay, I'll come get you when he arrives." It works!

What is it that you're dreaming of today? That you're afraid to hope for? That you secretly desire, but haven't spoken into the universe?

I challenge you to pray about it, visualize it, and thank God for it as if it has already come to pass. Then, speak it everywhere you go and sit back and watch as God moves people and things miraculously in place to make your dreams come true.

What About Supply And Demand?

When I first began writing daily inspirational nuggets, I wondered who in the world might want to read them. Though I knew I was following my spirit as closely as I could – down to the time of day that I should write – I still doubted there was a need for yet another inspirational writer.

Surely, you know how it is when doubt sets in about something God has placed on your heart?

As many folks in publishing will advise you to do, I combed through my home library to find books I thought were similar to my writing style/idea. Two authors stood out: Susan Taylor and Iyanla Vanzant. "Wow, I'm in good company," I thought to myself.

Unfortunately, within a few moments, my thoughts switched from the positive to the negative as I found myself thinking, "If the two of them exist – plus countless others who haven't yet made a name for themselves, why is there a need for me?"

The mind is such a powerful and wonderful tool; especially when used against ourselves. From that initial negative thought, my mind spiraled into triple negative overtime. "Well, of course folks want to read their books. They're Susan and Iyanla! They're noted authors from Essence magazine, public speakers, motivational writers, and teachers extraordinaire. How can I even compare?"

This train was spiraling out of control really fast, so I struggled to reel myself back in. Was I able to switch back to my positive thinking? Not exactly. Instead, I tried to convince myself I was writing just for the love of it, without thought as to whether anyone might ever read it. I'll just write because I enjoy it!

Now, this is a lofty goal, and one that I recommend to anyone following their passion. "Do what you love and you'll never work a day in your life," says Dennis Kimbro. "Your passion is that thing you'd do, even if you never got paid for it," say countless others. I believe these things with all of my heart, but to say that I'm writing without thought of anyone ever reading it is a pile of crap! Of course, I want someone to read what I've written – in the same way you'd want your movie seen if you were a filmmaker, your clothes shown as a designer, your music heard as a composer/producer, your speeches heard if you were a public speaker.... In fact, I was just scared to hope that I was good enough at my craft.

Worse yet, I was comparing my own goals to those of others in my field, and afraid somehow I'd come up short.

As I reflected on these things, what came to mind is what God has for me, is just for me. I've heard that saying a thousand times, but not until this very moment did I fully ingest what that means. In sum, it means scoot over Susan and Iyanla, you've got company!

Or, put another way, God does not deal in lack when he assigns purpose and destiny. He doesn't place on our hearts desires that can only be filled for the first 10 in line, with us standing in position number 11. He doesn't order our steps in ways that will lead to our frustration when we get there and see that the need is already fulfilled. No! There is a special void in this world that only you can meet.

That line of thinking is true as it relates to the purpose God gave you, but also works for every Godly desire. If it's your job, stop looking around at who else is applying. Your job is your job! If it's your man, stop looking around at other women who are interested. Your man is your man! What God has for you, is just for you. And, while you're at it (single women), stop counting how many men there are in relation to the number of women. Why does it matter if there's only ten men? You only need your one, right? What's for you, is for you! God put just enough of ___ into the universe with your name on it, so stop sweating!

Taking it one step further, maybe if we realize that God's supply is unlimited, we'll stop trying to hold onto things we know aren't ours in this season. You know how we do. Just in case our ideal thing doesn't come along, we hold on to what we've got in the meantime. Hey, I'm speaking for everyone else when I say, if you're trying to hold on to my blessing, let it go and stop trying to hold up my progress! It's much easier if you let go voluntarily; because if God makes you turn it loose, it could be a lot less comfortable.

In the same vein, stop being afraid to share resources because of a fear of lack. People always marveled that when I was in law school, I'd share my notes/outlines with anyone who asked. Why? Because I didn't care if everyone got an A, as long as I got one. That's why I love it today when I meet authors who are happy to pass on publishing contacts without acting as if the publisher might stop printing books after they are done with mine, or as if having another book on the shelves will threaten their livelihood. Because it's a testament to the notion that there is enough.

Today, where ever you are, take a moment to affirm that what God has for you, is just for you. So, you need not compare yourself to others, hold tight to things that are not right, or be afraid to share resources because of fear there isn't enough to go around. Before you were formed in the womb, God worked it all out just for you.

God, I thank you right now that you are boundless and your supply is infinite. I thank you that when you created the desires of my heart, you also created a need in the world to complement them. Thank you for removing the fear of lack, and for reminding me that you are the ultimate source.

Amen.

What About Adaptation?

There's usually at least one scene in a movie that stays with me long after the credits roll. One of my all-time favorites comes from "Adaptation," an off-color movie starring Nicholas Cage. Nicholas plays two characters – an extremely introverted, overanalyzing writer who is afraid to show his emotions; and his very extroverted, "anything goes," always lovable brother.

In one of the movie's critical scenes, the introvert is asking the extrovert how he could have openly loved a woman who treated him horribly and didn't love him back. The extrovert thinks for a moment, then utters words that I'll never forget. He says something like this:

"It was my choice to love her, because the love was mine to give. . . . But, what she did with the love, well, that was up to her."

Of course, it was much more dramatic when Nicholas said it in the context of the movie, but hopefully the point comes through. Here was a man happy to give his love without reservation, because that was what made him feel good. Period.

I've often thought of that scene in the romantic context, but this morning, for the first time, I found myself thinking about it from a different perspective. I imagined this fictional character being tormented by a woman who treated him like crap, yet managing to stay in a place of love. Putting aside the question of whether he was in a healthy relationship and all that jazz, I found myself wondering why it isn't always this simple, not just with romantic love, but in everyday life?

Have you ever gotten up in the morning feeling great and envisioning a day full of peace, but then those feelings dissipate as you step outside your house, while you're driving, or as you enter your workplace?

The crazy driver who rudely speeds up so you can't get over . . . the rude salesperson who acts like you're an imposition . . . demons all up and through your workplace. . . . I don't know how you respond, but for me, with each incident, I often find my peaceful, loving spirit being chipped away. By the end of the day, I'm driving home in some mad road rage, wishing I had rubber bumpers so that I could really show them who they're messing with! Come on, don't act like I'm the only one who has ever wished they could just ram into the idiot on the road to teach them a lesson?

My point? Why do we let others have so much power over us? Why do we let people and situations move us from our loving place? Why do we let other people's 'stuff' cause us to be in a funk?

Why can't we just choose to stay in good cheer, no matter what's thrown our way – giving love, without thought as to what the other person will choose to do with it?

Want the hard, cold truth? We can. But, sometimes we choose not to. Yep, that's right. It's completely up to us whether we adapt to our surroundings, or whether we adapt our surroundings to us.

Take for example, an attorney with whom I used to work. There were times when he approached me with an attitude of negativity and anger. As he grew more animated, I had a choice. I could have responded in anger, and tried to be the one who puffed my chest out and yelled the loudest. But instead, I took a deep breath, found my center, and calmly provided the information he needed. Guess what happened? His tone softened, his voice lowered, and he found a more peaceful center too. It was pretty amazing. Felt almost like my being kind had shined a spotlight on how crazy he was acting, and he couldn't maintain it alone.

In the same way, I've 'adapted my surroundings to me' as I encountered rude strangers. It may not work with everyone, but you'll be surprised to find out how much hate a genuine smile can melt through.

Granted, we might not always walk around smiling and laughing, because there are days when that may be asking too much.

But, consider this: Those times when you're walking around feeling funky or angry or mad at the world, you do so by choice. Those times when you internalize and build upon negativity that's thrown your way by a friend, a co-worker, or even a stranger; you do so by choice.

Next time someone or something tries to steal your peace, remember that you can adapt to your surroundings, or you can adapt your surroundings to you.

The choice is yours.

What About Our Path?

Do you trust your intuition?

One of the hardest things I've had to learn is how to listen to my inner spirit. The lessons started with really small things – like me noticing my phone charger plugged in the wall as I leave my house, but not going back to get it; then later beating myself up when I realized I should have brought it because my battery was low. Seemingly silly things like that.

Then, as I listened more, I found myself saying things like, "I don't know why I took the back roads instead of I-20. It's not that I expected a massive pile-up on the freeway. For some reason, going this way just *felt* right." Or, "I can't explain why I told the stranger next to me at the theater that I'm a writer. I just followed my gut. Now I'm glad I did because she turned out to be a valuable connection."

I noticed the same inner voice – which I know to be from God – would help lead me on every decision in my life – whether it was something small, like which way to drive into work; or something larger, like whether a certain professional move was the right one for me.

Though I still struggle sometimes to listen and follow, I'm much better now about doing the things that "feel right to my spirit," even if I'm sometimes unable to explain my reasons to anyone else. Every day, I become more in tune with what God is telling me and I get better at following what I hear without reservation.

But, there are those other times when I find myself still agonizing over a decision I have to make, or wondering if a decision I already made was the right one.

Haven't you ever found yourself questioning the "right" move?

With me, I find that my mind goes into a tailspin that starts something like this: Is this the *right* agent for me? The *right* publishing house? The *right* deal? Maybe I should have . . . .

Is this person the *right* one for me to date? Or, should I nip this in the bud now?

Was the person I married *wrong*? Did I miss something God was telling me?

Should I have gone to law school, or would I have been better off moving to New York to become a writer and editor? Why didn't I do it then?

Maybe you've reached the ultimate level of contentment and have no clue what I'm talking about, but my brain sometimes just won't give it a rest! I still torture myself with many decisions, questioning which path is "right" and which one is "wrong." I worry that I'll choose the wrong one.

But not today.

This morning I'm remembering the last time I beat myself up over a small, but not insignificant, "wrong" decision I made. It was one of those days when I obviously didn't listen to my spirit saying to take the back roads instead of the freeway in to work. As luck would have it, I found myself in bumper to bumper traffic, struggling to get to work by 9 a.m. for a weekly conference call. I beat up on myself for not going the *right* way, and imagined all sorts of plagues falling down upon me because I was late. All because I went the *wrong* way.

Then, a funny thing happened. I finally made it to work, feeling stressed and concerned. Hurriedly, I parked my car and almost ran to the elevators and up into my office. I then quickly logged onto the call and announced my arrival to my co-workers.

It was about five minutes after 9.

Not only was my slight tardiness not a big deal, but the call hadn't even really started. I wasn't even the last one to arrive.

Why had I tortured myself over a decision I made, only to find I'd ended up in the exact same place?

Why do we beat ourselves up – literally, agonizing over whether to go left or right, backwards or forward; without realizing that any move we prayerfully make will land us exactly where we're supposed to be?

Don't you see?

I agonized over whether I married the right person. But, God took the decision I made and caused something beautiful to come from it. If I hadn't chosen him, I wouldn't have had the experiences on which to begin writing. That decision – whether I label it as "right" or "wrong" – landed me in the *right* place.

I agonized over whether I should have gone to law school or moved to New York for a career in writing. But, some might argue that I just took the scenic route – filled with useful experiences – to the editing and writing career I considered fifteen years ago. I would also argue that I landed here at a better time, and more prepared for the task at hand.

Is there a decision you have to make that's causing you anxiety? Or, a decision you made that you've been beating up on yourself about because you think it may have been *wrong*? If so, stop right where you are.

Just stop.

Remind yourself that your steps are divinely ordered. That means if you prayerfully move forward, there will be no *wrong* moves. If you remain prayerful, God will place you in the exact place you need to be at the precise moment you need to be there.

Trust and believe. The path may not seem clear to you. In fact, it may sometimes feel as if you're on a plane ride with lots of really long layovers. But, if you just trust and believe, you'll reach your destination at the perfect, appointed time.

What's more, you may just find that you're all the better because of the experiences you collected along the way.

What About The Rain?

This morning I woke up to the sound of rain outside my window. "What a way to start the week," I thought, as I pulled a pillow over my head and decided not to get up to write. "Perfect sleep-in weather, and besides, traffic is probably going to be awful!"

But, as I reclaimed my comfortable position and tried to doze off, I listened again.

This time, I heard the sound of God washing away all of the pollen that's been making so many of us miserable.

This time, I envisioned God pouring a tall glass of water for all of his creations that have been dying of thirst, mainly because of what we're doing to the environment.

This time, I could have sworn I heard my car breathe a huge sigh of relief that someone had come to its rescue with a nature provided bath, since I surely haven't taken it to the car wash in ages.

Finally, I listened, and I smiled as I thought of God washing away all of the not so great things of yesterday, last week, and the past years; to give me a brand new, unblemished day.

What would you wash away if you could?

Are there decisions you've made, that despite your knowing logically that God will fix, you still think of with regret? Hurt feelings or anger from something someone did or said to you that despite your best self therapy still brings about a familiar pain? Unforgiveness that you haven't been able to pray away, or maybe something for which you need to be forgiven?

Or, perhaps it isn't even that complex. Maybe last week was just a crappy week for which you'd like to have a "do over."

As I listened to the sound of the rain on my window pane, I realized today is a new day, full of new opportunities. I can be the person who makes healthy choices about eating and works out at lunch. I can get to work early, be more productive, and be a better financial steward. I can let go of things of the past that may be holding me back and move into a new future. I can be a better mentor and friend, and just an all around better me.

Today, I can choose to expect the miracle I've been waiting on, and have faith that today might be the perfect anointed time.

Today, is a new day full of infinite possibilities.

I woke up this morning to the sound of pouring rain, and I heard God giving out second chances; taking away hurt, regret and anger; doling out forgiveness and forgiving spirits; and giving free "reset" buttons for our lives.

Listen closely. Can you hear it? It's the sound of a fresh start.

Isn't it beautiful?

What About Miracles?

Dear God,

Every day I wake up expecting a miracle.

As I get dressed for work and make the drive in, I pray that today is the day when things move in a way that will give me the desires of my heart: perfect health, perfect love, a vocation that is purposeful and prosperous, <u>and</u> the same blessings for my family and friends. And, as I park my car and literally drag myself into the office, I pray for a breakthrough and I thank you in expectation of your grace.

But, today was different. Today, when I woke up, I asked you for nothing. Instead, I just sat back and observed.

Here's what I saw.

You allowed me to wake up, as the old folks used to say, in my "right" mind, which I know isn't guaranteed.

You gave me "perfect" health to get up without assistance. You gave me the means to dress myself in clothes that not only keep me warm, but do so with some flair. You allowed my car to start, though it's advancing in years, and got me to the gas station although my gauge showed I was on "E."

You gave me the funds to fill up my gas tank, despite gas prices being at an all-time high. You guided my car into the office safely. When I got there, you reminded me that this job that provides for all of my needs and many of my wants is exactly where you have purposed me to be.

You gave me free Krispy Kreme donuts for breakfast, and surrounded me with love (by email and phone) from my friends and family. You showed me they were safe and taken care of. You gave me a smile and put enough joy in my heart to share with my co-worker who looked like she was in need.

Though I know you told me the desires of my heart would be given to me if I delight in you – just for today, as I continue forward with a day that was not promised, I choose not to ask you for anything.

Instead, today I just thank you for the miracles you show me each and every day.

What About Putting First Things First?

This morning I got up in a huff, worried about all the things that need to get done before I leave for Spain in 36 hours and counting. I hurriedly prayed about the topic of my inspirational nugget. After a quick prayer, what came to me is that I should write about "putting first things first."

As I continued to pray, I began writing about the difficulties I was having in finding enough hours in the day to do all the things I need to do before I leave, especially with new "emergencies" cropping up at every turn.

When I finished writing, I felt unfamiliar discomfort about my topic, but I shrugged it aside. After all, work was waiting.

Just then my cell phone rang.

Despite the early hour I tried to convince myself that it was good news. But, as soon as I heard the tremor in my girlfriend's voice, I knew that something was wrong. Through intermittent sobs, she told me she'd gotten a call that morning to tell her that a loved one passed away. He'd had a heart attack during the night and transitioned early this morning.

I tried to offer words of comfort, and we talked about our collective relief that he didn't suffer long. She talked about making time now to plan a trip back home for the services and to visit other family.

That's when it hit me. In that single moment, I realized what God meant when he told me to write about putting first things first. Sure, he was telling me to prioritize my own getaway time, but more than that, he was telling me to prioritize all of the things and people that should matter most in my life.

For months my friend had been postponing a trip to see her loved one. We'd talked about it several times and I'd cautioned that tomorrow is never promised. But, it was never the right time to go. There were a variety of very legitimate and compelling reasons to put it off. The distance made the trip one that didn't make sense for just a weekend, so at the end of the day, she'd decided to visit him later this year.

That had been the plan.

Hearing my girlfriend's story made me question my own priorities, and leads me to ask:

What have you put onto the back burner for another day? What "first things" in your life have been put last because of all of the seemingly important things going on in your life?

It could be something big like traveling to see a loved one or friend. Or, something that may seem small, like taking a vacation to get away and recharge, or doing something else just for you. It could even be something that seems minute, like taking a moment in your day to pick up the phone to say "I love you."

There are always going to be things that you think of as having to get done: projects to complete, bills to pay, life to live . . . . But, there won't always be a loved one to call. And, if you don't take care of yourself first – prioritizing your own time to recharge – you won't have to worry about getting all of those things done, because there won't be a you to do them.

I realize it's easier said than done when real life issues are pulling at every turn, making it seem as if there are not enough hours in the day. But, you know what? Somehow, if you put the most important things first, the other things always work out in time.

Just for today, see the unimportant things as what they really are: insignificant.

And, see the people, moments, and events in your life as what they really are: irreplaceable.

Thank you, God, for helping me prioritize my life, and for giving me another opportunity to put first things first.

What About Angels?

Several weeks ago I became somewhat discouraged as I realized that I had yet to receive the miracle I'd been expecting. You know how we do: we pray about things like relationships, finances, career changes (aka "purpose"), and health; and sometimes feel as if no matter how many steps we take, we don't move forward. Though we appreciate the "little" miracles that propel us through each day, we sometimes still long for that really big one that feels just beyond our reach.

I moped around for days without any real answers or breakthroughs.

Then, as I continued to pray, I had an epiphany. I knew what I had to do. I had the distinct vision of writing a check to one of my friends who I knew had been praying for her finances. Despite coming up with many logical reasons not to do so, I took out my checkbook and wrote out the amount I'd seen during my prayers.

My thought? We shouldn't just expect a miracle. Instead, we should strive to BE a miracle.

What happened next confirmed my belief that God can use us all as angels. Soon after receiving the check, my friend expressed her appreciation, along with pure shock that I had given the money during her exact time of need. What was more amazing is that it was the EXACT amount for which she'd been praying. We were both moved to tears.

She received her miracle, and I felt good in helping to create one.

The story doesn't end there.

Today, I woke up and prepared for my flight from Barcelona to Rome, while praying about the next steps on a project. I was torn about what to do, and unsure if I was on the right path.

When I checked my email I was amazed to learn that a new friend sowed a blessing for me. I won't go into details here, but it was an act of pure kindness without expectation. When I learned of it, I was overwhelmed at the gesture, then completely blown away as I stopped and realized something remarkable.

My friend's act of kindness came at the exact right time to answer my prayers about confirming I'm on the right path. Even more amazingly, it included a gift in the EXACT amount that I'd previously given to my other friend.

My miracle came back to me.

Where is it written that God's work is done only by his hands, without the assistance of his earthly angels? In fact, aren't we all God's angels waiting to mobilize?

Have you taken time to create a miracle for someone else, or, like me, have you been more consumed with your own prayer requests?

Today I challenge you: whatever it is you're praying for, stop right where you are in asking, and GIVE. Give the thing you've been wanting or the thing someone else may need. Be the miracle you're expecting.

I guarantee that if you do, you will restore someone else's belief in angels, as you restore your own.

What About Being Plugged In?

Have you ever wondered where peace comes from? I'm not just talking about the peace that fills your spirit when you know you're in the right place at the right time, or when life is skittles and rainbows. I mean peace that soothes your soul during those *other* times. Whether it's a catastrophic, life changing event; or just one of those days when your patience is tested. What makes us able to be all "Zen" sometimes, and just completely lose it in others?

This was one of the questions that came to mind as I was traveling across Europe. Every day I noted things that typically might push me out of my peace zone – a lengthy flight delay, a long wait for luggage, rude people trampling over me as I made my way onto the train, hustlers trying to rip me off, bad service . . . . The list goes on and on. But, despite it all, I had the trip of a lifetime. If the flight or luggage was delayed, I thanked God that I had nowhere I had to be. If someone tried to walk over me, I laughed at the culture and matched their aggression. If someone "accidentally" miscounted my change, I prayed that it would help them in their time of need. And, for the occasional bad server who didn't want to be bothered with simple non-Spanish speaking Americans, I kept smiling until I won them over. (Or, at least, I tried!)

My peace would not be moved.

At first, I explained it away as me being in vacation mode, where I let things roll off my back. But, this morning as I think back, I realize that my peace had little to do with my being on vacation and nothing to do with where I was located.

I was at peace because I was plugged in. That is, I looked inward instead of outward to ground me. Because my peace came from within, I wasn't affected by things of the world in the same way.

How many times have you based your peace on what happened during a work day, on how your boss or co-workers treated you, or better yet, on a traffic-laden drive into work? Or, perhaps on a mate or friend who you expected to make things ok? Or, maybe on certain financial expectations that may or may not have come through?

How many times have things in and of the world seemed to destroy your peace?

For me, the answer used to be almost daily. But now that my little excursion has reminded me of the true source of everything, including the secret of my contentment, my goal is to remain connected to the Source each and every day.

I can't say that it will always be easy, or that I'll always remember how to regain my peace. But, now that I know the secret of contentment, I know what to do.

Next time things of the world threaten to consume you, stop right where you are and just plug in.

What About Lack?

A few days ago I heard someone use the "R" word.

Although I knew it was lingering out there, I avoided it for as long as possible. I changed the channel during news briefs, ignored headlines on the Internet, and avoided any discussions. But, finally, it caught up with me, as I heard someone say that our country is in a Recession.

Now you know how I feel about the power of words! I'm a huge believer in "I think; therefore I am." Or, in biblical terms, "There's power of life and death in the tongue." So, you probably understand why the word Recession sent a chill down my spine. My mind started spinning with thoughts of job security (or lack thereof) and I started questioning some of my recent expenditures (Europe wasn't exactly cheap). Even gas began to feel more expensive as I started wondering if I should stay home more and drive less.

But, then I heard my own voice saying the 3 little words I'd given to a friend just days before: *there is enough.*

Those are the words I repeated time and time again when she seemed fearful about how things would work out financially. Of course, when talking to her, I was cool and confident, so the words easily rolled off my tongue. But when I heard the "R" word for myself, it hit closer to home. For a moment my words seemed shallow and fear began to seep in.

Am I the only one having these thoughts?

You know the thoughts that make you start mentally tallying your rainy day accounts, then make you pray that the sun shines long enough for you to get a real rainy day account as opposed to the little drizzle account you currently have? I have to admit that in an extreme moment, I wanted to start counting my pennies and growing vegetables in my backyard!

Until I remembered why there's enough. Why there will always be enough. Why I've never gone hungry, or without a place to lay my head. Why I'm always clothed and taken care of. Why anything I've lost has always been replaced with something ten times better.

Quite simply, there's enough because God's supply is infinite.

I mean, think about it. Have you ever gone hungry? Even in your worst moment, hasn't something always broken to provide you with what you needed, and many times with what you wanted too?

In the coming months, I suspect we'll hear more about this so-called Recession. Folks will clutch their purses tighter, stay closer to home, and worry more. But, I hope you'll resist going with the masses.

Knowing that God's supply is infinite, I hope you'll keep your hand open to give to those in need.

Knowing that God's supply is infinite, I hope you'll still dare to follow the purpose placed in your heart, even if that dream seems less practical than some think prudent.

Knowing that God's supply is infinite, I hope you'll trust God to provide for you, just as he always has.

In fact, the next time you hear the word Recession, I hope you'll consider replacing it with some R words of your own:

Reap

Reward

Renew

Replenish

Revive

Regenerate

Revitalize

Refill

Restore

Those are the only R words I want to manifest in my life. Knowing the Source of all things makes me feel confident that I will, and that you will too.

What About One Day At A Time?

Amazing.

It has been weeks since I last got up early to spend my quiet time with God. I made up excuses (such as getting back on this time zone), felt bad about it (but still couldn't seem to get it together), and gave vague answers in response to questions about when my thoughts of the day would resume ("Well, I never actually said they'd be EVERY day").

I set my alarm last night, determined this week would be better. I didn't vow to wake up every day, but instead decided to commit to just today, then take it one day at a time.

I was so excited that I woke up before the alarm. In fact, I was wide awake when I looked at the clock and realized that it was only 3 a.m. I was early, which isn't at all like my norm. But, something inside me said "get on up" so I pulled the computer to my lap and decided to give it a whirl.

Before the new document opened, I had words. First one sentence, and then a paragraph, and then pages that just dripped from me. The feeling was so good that I wondered what took me so long to return.

Then I knew. I was almost ashamed to admit it but I knew then that the thing that had kept me away for so long was fear.

I knew what I should have been doing. There wasn't a doubt in my mind that the early morning writing time was divinely inspired. Yet, despite knowing, I fell short. Every time I thought about going back, my guilt made me fear that it wouldn't be the same. Funny how I sometimes forget that he's not petty like us.

Have you ever had God place something on your heart that you didn't do?

Well, if it's any consolation, when I woke up this morning, I could swear that I heard him whisper in my ear these words:

"I'm always here. You're right on time."

Then he told me it's okay that I don't always do what I should, when I should. He reminded me that all we can do is try to do better each and every day.

We move about doing the various things in our life that seem pressing. We go here and there, sometimes forgetting to even look back. But when we do, sure enough, he's still right there. If we just open our eyes, we'll see that he's not just *there*, but everywhere. He's in the office when folks start cutting up – and when we miraculously finish the project that seemed impossible. He's running with me when I feel like I can't take another step. He's there in the still of the night when no one else is around to give me a hug. I just sometimes forget to reach and out and touch him.

I can't promise that I'm going to get up early every morning to write; nor do I know how long these writings will continue. But, I do promise this: I'm going to do better on finding that quiet time with him because I know he placed this on my heart, and I know that I'm better for it. Actually, I'm going to do better on following through on ALL of the things that he's placed on my heart.

When I fall off the wagon, as I undoubtedly will, I'm not going to let fear keep me away for so long because I know that when I return, he'll be right there, telling me . . .

"I'm always here. You're right on time."

Won't you join me?

What About Addiction?

Last night I had to have some twizzlers. Yes, I mean "had to" – as if twizzlers were the very thing my life depended on.

It was really quite sad in hindsight because my intense craving came not 15 minutes after my new resolve to rid my body of any toxic treats for at least a week, and literally years after my last "fix." (Yes, I am a recovering twizzlerholic. Fourteen months; twenty six days; 3 hours and 10 minutes.) I hadn't even missed them . . . until I did. When I did, it was like an internal war inside of me. I'd even gone on a 6 mile run/walk to seal the deal of eating healthy. But, obviously, some part of my body wanted out.

I ate grapes to try to tame the beast.

Drank a cup of juice.

Thought about my workout goals. (After all, who wants to look bloated on Oprah?)

But, my body was relentless. As I looked for where I'd put the bag of twizzlers given to me days before as a gift (and untouched), I compared myself to Samuel Jackson in New Jack City. ("I'm gonna do the dance, mama!"). Then immediately felt bad for making comedic swipes at a crack addict. This was pretty bad.

Finally, twizzlers bag in hand, with one dangling from my mouth like a cigarette, it dawned on me that it wasn't twizzlers I was craving.

I wanted something to make me feel good – to give me pleasure that for whatever reason I seemed to be at that very moment missing. Wanted to indulge in that thing that would wrap me in happiness and make me forget that in just a few hours it would be time to start the grind of another work week at a job that I was (though immensely grateful for) not happy to return to. Somehow those twizzlers were going to help me chew my way through the meantime and give me the satisfaction I'd been searching for.

Except, they didn't.

When I looked back down, in shock I might add, at the empty bag that somebody had polished off while I wasn't looking, I realized they weren't really that good. You have to chew too much; they get stuck in your teeth; and they're not juicy or filled with flavor.

Worst of all; an entire bag later and I was in exactly the same place as I'd started. Hours away from going to *that job*. The one I love to hate; and hate so much I can't love. The one I'm immensely thankful for because I have to be. The one I envision leaving in a variety of ways – from winning the lotto, to the call from O's studio, to some (at this point completely random) man who says, "Baby, just quit, I'll take care of you!"

What was I doing? How could I do better, before ending up as the 600 pound associate?

Certainly you have twizzlers in your life?

What do you do when you feel angst about an area of your life that's missing something? Is there something that you try, only to realize that you don't feel any better than before you started? Eat? Drink? Have sex? Shop? Call friends instead of taking quiet time to listen? Hide in someone else's world (i.e. TV or movies) so as not to focus on your own?

I don't know what your twizzlers are, but I think we all have them at times in our lives. Step one, I think, is admitting the problem. Put the spotlight on it and see it for what it is! Step two, I think, is addressing the root of the problem. Take a moment to look inside to figure out what void (if any) you're trying to fill. Then know that the Source of wholeness can heal any wound, and cure any addiction.

God, right now I thank you for helping me identify any addictions in my life – those that are apparent and those that are buried a little deeper. I pray that you fill those empty places in ways that alleviate the need for any vice. And, I thank you in advance, knowing that it is done.

What About Love?

Love.

I feel like Carrie Bradshaw. Wanting to write something, but with only one word that comes to mind. But, maybe this four letter word is more than enough.

I've been thinking a lot lately about love. What it is. Why some people find it so easily and others of us seem to spend our whole lives searching. Wondering if while we're searching, we might miss out on the love that's right before our eyes.

I joke a lot about it, but the truth is I have absolutely no idea if I'll get married again.

Is it possible that some of us are wired differently, and that isn't how we'll best grow and learn our lessons?

Possible that instead of sitting on the porch holding hands with the man of my dreams when I'm ninety, I'll be sitting next to one of my girls cackling about something we did back in the day?

Imagine my surprise when I realized that my longest sustained relationship has been with another girl! Twenty years and counting. That's how long we've been "married." She listens when I've had a bad day; shares in my joys when something good happens; and holds my hand through the really bad spells. And, of course, like a man, every now and again it feels like we're speaking two different languages and we get on each other's last nerve!

Hey, if God created women who complement me, support me, nurture me, and just plain old "get me," then why do I doubt that he created such a man? If I can sustain a healthy, loving friendship with a woman for 20 years, then why do I doubt that I can have the same (also with romance and passion of course) with a man?

Love.

What About Now?

This morning I woke up without the usual thoughts about what God would have me to write. No situation I've been through came to mind. No questions for me to answer. Instead, I found myself with a single question for God.

What would you have me to do now?

I know that's about as broad of a question as they come. Not, "What would you have me to do about x or y or z?" Just a question as vague as someone who feels they are blindly making their way through a dark forest and is granted one question, but who doesn't want to be so specific as to say, "Should I go left or right," because at that point the answer could be up or down or sideways. So instead, he just says, *"What now, God?"*

See, I've been coasting along fairly well for the past several weeks, even though I've been quietly doing so. Haven't had any major breakthroughs personally or professionally, but I've maintained more peace than not. I've even stopped calling this "the meantime," because let's face it, that's what life is. We bounce from peak to peak in our lives, and in between is where we do the real living. No, calling it "the meantime" is a misnomer and keeps us strung out waiting on the next high, so we don't see the beauty of every step in between.

But, what now, God?

I'm appreciating the moments much more than I ever have, living life more fully and finding contentment in areas of my life where I desire change. I'm letting go of things I thought I wanted and trusting God to provide what I need. (I don't think I published any writings on marriage and kids, so I'll sum it up by saying that for the first time in my life I'm okay if that's not in my plan. Of course, I reserve the right to change my mind next week!). I'm even accepting that God's timeline is divine, such that I've stopped walking around waiting for an agent, publisher, or even O's people's people to call. God placed the desire to write on my heart and I'm doing my part, so the rest will be what it should be when it's time.

So, if I'm so highly evolved (and "Zen," as I like to call it), why do I still feel as if I'm missing a piece of the puzzle?

Because for years I've been wired to believe that we're in constant pursuit of the greener grass. When it's all said and done, I don't know how to stop looking for the next thing.

Because I still want so many things that have yet to manifest. I don't know what to do with those desires. Even with faith that they will come at the anointed time and appointed season, I still long for . . . more.

Because I don't want to get complacent, I guess. I don't want to look up 10 years from now and find that I ended up settling for a job I never really liked, a man who is almost what I wanted, and a life that bears little resemblance to what I've dreamed about. Because I'm scared that if I don't keep waiting on the right phone call, or looking for the real Prince Charming, that maybe they'll never come.

So how do I find the balance between living in a place of contentment and patience, and manifesting the things I still feel God promised?

That's when I heard God say, "That's when it becomes about faith."

As one of my friends once said, you put your prayer requests into your "something for Jesus to do" box. Then you simply let go.

Being human, you may peek in the box every now and again to make sure it's still there. You may remind God that you put it there, because you worry that he's forgotten (although he never will). You may even take it out and revise it from time to time because sometimes our desires change. But when it's all said and done, you drop it in, close the lid tightly, and you walk away.

What now, God?

"Nothing. Absolutely nothing. You've done your part. Now you can do nothing as I do mine."

What About Letting Go?

I want to be one of those people who happily run to embrace change.

Change is good. Change is my friend. Change is where much of our growth and blessings come from. Right?

Then, why is change so scary?

This past weekend, I went to a family reunion on my dad's side. I saw family members that I hadn't seen in over a decade, so of course, everyone was in a different place than I remembered. But, the biggest change I saw was a bit closer to home.

At the last reunion, my mom walked in with her head held high. She greeted each relative with a smile, shared a laugh or two, and seemed to genuinely enjoy herself.

At this reunion, my sisters and I wheeled my mom in and watched as many well-meaning cousins yelled at her or talked to her as if she were two years old. As if being in a wheelchair meant that she could no longer hear or comprehend. True enough, Parkinson's Disease can slow everything down, but I cringed each time someone acted as if my mom wasn't there. Each time they asked me how "she" was doing, while completely ignoring that "she" was sitting there, fully capable of responding on her own.

As my sisters and I helped my mom undress each night and tucked her in to bed, I couldn't help but to marvel at the cycle of life and change. Who knew I'd live to see the day when I tucked my mom in, instead of the other way around?

Haven't you ever been in a place in your life where you didn't want things to change? When you wanted to press pause, or even rewind, so that you could hold on to things as they were?

I have.

But, this morning, as I prayed, the vision I had was of my hand balled into a fist, holding tightly to something. For the first time, instead of focusing on what I was holding onto, I focused on the things that couldn't get in.

I envisioned myself holding onto my mother, instead of releasing her (when it's her time) to the next realm, which I believe to be free of pain or ailment. A place where she doesn't need a wheelchair.

I envisioned myself holding on to relationships of the past (both romantic and platonic) that no longer serve my greater good, and some that perhaps never did; while someone infinitely better, more healthy, reciprocal, loving, and perfect passes me by.

I envisioned myself holding tightly to a job that I've outgrown, out of fear; while a prosperous, purpose-filled, passionate profession lies just beyond my grasp – and I need only extend my hand to grab it.

As I opened my hand in my mind's eye, I had a startling realization. I realized that the things I've held onto so tightly don't even fit anymore. Nor, do they compare with the blessings to come. I also realized that holding onto things is never a good idea, because we can hold them so tightly they don't have room to grow. It's like the old saying, set it free and if it's yours, it will return to you. Infinitely better.

What are you holding onto tightly in your hand today? Are you holding on out of fear of change, or fear that it won't return to you? If so, let it go. And, as you open your hand to let it go, thank God for what he lets in.

What About The Between Time?

This morning I woke up at 4 a.m. for prayer and meditation, but instead of going right to the computer, I decided to go downstairs to grab something to drink. As I left out of my room, I was shocked and amazed to see my girlfriend – who is staying with me – looking as awake as if it were 4 p.m. When I asked what she was doing up, she shrugged and dispassionately said, "work."

A number of things went through my mind, but I said nothing. I thought of all of the times that I've worked crazy hours to meet the demands of a job that sometimes gets on my last nerve. And, how different that is from the joy I feel at staying up late to write. My eyes locked with my friend's, and without words, we both "said" the same thing: "How long before we get through this to something better?"

As I thought about it more, I realized this was a recurring question for me – my mind had been grappling all week with thoughts about unanswered prayers. Not just things that I've been personally praying on, but also prayers that I've joined in on with those close to me. You know, the same basic things that most of us are looking for: better jobs, better relationships, better finances . . . .

As I thought about waiting on these things to manifest, I heard my own voice saying that there is no "meantime," because if we live for the next big thing, we'll wish our lives away without enjoying the moments. Yet, despite knowing that to be true, I couldn't help but to wonder, how do we patiently wait for our breakthrough?

In other words, what about the time between when we pray with faith that could move mountains, and the time that we see the mountain has actually moved?

For me, I have to admit that there have been times when the period in between my prayer being uttered and my mountain being affected has seemed like an eternity! It has been 7 years since my divorce and more than 10 years that I've been talking about a different profession, which means that I've been praying for several years for the right relationship and the right job, but alas, I'se still here! Working for the man, and not having found a man – or at least, not the right one.

So, if this isn't "the meantime," what is it?

I prayed and asked God to show me – tell me something that would help this time make sense. As I prayed, I thought back on the past several years from a different vantage point. I thought about what would have happened if God had sent me my mate, even three years ago when I thought I was ready. Much as I hated to admit it, I wasn't even close. I wanted to be ready; I thought I was ready; and I couldn't understand why God didn't give me the desires of my heart that I prayed for so earnestly. But, the truth was, there was some real growing that I needed to do first.

Similarly, I'm thinking about what would have happened if God had let me publish the book I was trying to write back then. If I pulled out a draft now, I'd probably cringe at what crap it was. I thought it was good at the time, but now? Now I'm so glad that I didn't run out and self-publish or otherwise rush the process. There were more lessons I needed to learn before I could tell my story in a way that would help someone else.

And, my finances? Well, if God had given me a windfall of money back in the day, I hate to admit it, but I might nonetheless be financially strapped today. Why? Because I wasn't a good financial steward with the $2 he gave me. What made me think that getting $2 million would make me any better? I needed time to learn how to save and to spend wisely so that I'd be a better vessel.

Of course there's time between when we send up our prayers, and when God answers them. Much as I hate to admit it, there simply has to be. It's not that God needs time to make it so. Manifesting our desires could be as easy as rubbing on a Genie bottle. But, having our prayers answered at anything but the divinely perfect time would likely lead to disaster and we'd wind up looking lost, confused, and worse for it – kind of like

Jim Carrey in Bruce Almighty when he's playing God and messes up everything by immediately granting everyone's prayers.

God, today I thank you for the desires you've placed in my heart, for the period of preparation that makes me ready to receive them, for trust that you'll bring them at the perfect divine hour, and for peace and patience in the between times.

What About Sharing?

When I was a little girl, a saleslady once stopped me and said something like, "Oh my, do you know what pretty eyes you have?" With the honesty that only a three-year old can muster, I replied, "Yes, I do!"

My mother was probably completely embarrassed, and I'm sure she later explained to me that there are certain things you just don't say. As I grew older, the list of things you shouldn't do or say extended well beyond lessons in humility. In fact, by the time I was in the second grade, I'd become a much more inhibited and shy little girl. Not only was I more modest, but I understood that you should never impose on other people, and that private business just shouldn't be shared.

This week I've been thinking about the value of those lessons and how well they served me at different points in my life. But, I've also realized how my own interpretation of those lessons for many years hindered me.

Well into my adulthood, I was the person who only shared my faults, weaknesses, insecurities, and fears (if at all) with those closest to me. Until life threw me a curve ball and I found myself exposed. Losing a husband to mental illness with confessions of infidelity wasn't the worst thing for me. The absolute worst thing was having those things happen so publicly. Questioning what people would think or say at first consumed me . . . until a miraculous thing happened.

I was liberated.

With no place to run or hide, I was deliciously and deliriously free to be my wonderfully imperfect self. With this new freedom came something I'd never fully experienced before: an awareness that I'm not alone. Don't get me wrong, I've always felt the presence of God. But there were still times when I felt by myself in this earthly realm. Experiencing a sense of connection with other people was incredible and energizing.

It's the same feeling I've gotten this week after I wrote about my mother's illness. For every email I received marveling that I could expose such vulnerability; I received two more with stories of others who have gone through something similar or who just wanted to check on me. In these emails, I was able to talk to people who've walked in my shoes and who could show me by example that it gets better. I'd like to think that through these exchanges, we were all made stronger for having made that connection; a connection that never would have been made if not for us having the courage to show our vulnerabilities. I know that these exchanges were meant to show us that our vulnerabilities aren't so uncommon after all.

What have you kept close to the vest because you're afraid of what others might think?

I understand only too well how hard it can be to share the intimate details of your life, and how much trust it takes that the receiver will handle those details with care. Nonetheless, my prayer is that we'll all share more, connect more, and support more; and we'll be reminded that we're all in this thing together.

In the days to come, I challenge you to pull the rug off of some of the things you swept under it and ask for discernment on whose life you might bless by sharing. Also, conversely, I challenge you to ask someone how they're doing – how they're *really* doing – in a way that says you truly care.

No, this is not the part where I break out in singing "We Are The World." But, you know what? We really are. So, to the extent we haven't already, maybe we should start acting like it.

What About Being Still?

Someone asked me this morning when they would receive another one of my inspirational nuggets. My response was a gruff, "I have no idea!" Like everything else in my life, my writing appears to be at a standstill.

I thought more about the place I'm in as I showered and dressed for work. My mind filled with things I might should consider doing to move things forward. Should I be sending out more query letters to agents and publishers? Applying for more jobs in the meantime? Taking action in any other area of my life?

In the midst of my prayers, I felt the answer. Though I didn't like it one bit, I began to accept that sometimes we just have to be still.

Is there anything in your life you've been trying to push forward, only to find that you can't? Does it feel like you're pushing a giant boulder up a hill, but just barely able to sustain?

If so, maybe you should just stop and let go.

Letting go acknowledges that for as much as we like to believe we're in control, there are some things that are beyond our reach. I can send my book to 100 publishers, but until it reaches the right one at the right time, it's a lost cause.

By no means am I saying that we shouldn't work for what we want in our lives. After all, faith without works is nothing. I'm just saying that when you've done all you can do, let go and let God do the rest.

Then, just trust that he will.

What About A Sense Of Belonging?

Do you remember being a little kid, waiting to see if and when you'd be picked for a basketball or kickball game during gym class? I do. The pressure was so intense! I'd stand there, trying to act like I wasn't sweating it, while not being able to imagine a fate worse than being the last one standing. It didn't help any that I wasn't particularly athletic, was never team captain, and usually only had one really good friend who would pick me notwithstanding all of my shortcomings.

I realized this morning that I'm still that same little girl, standing by herself, hoping not to be the last one picked. Maybe I'm the only one, but even at times when I think I'm comfortable with being the 'singleton" amongst my friends who are married, there's still just a little piece of me that feels as if I'm waiting on a "team" to say "Oh, alright, I'll take her." In the meantime, I'm standing alone, feeling separate and apart from the rest. You won't see it when I walk down the street with my head held high, shoulders back, and looking like I haven't missed a beat. But, it's there.

Haven't you ever felt like you didn't belong?

Being single in a sea of married folks is just one way that I've sometimes felt like an outsider. In fact, there are all sorts of sororities in life that might make those of us who are not *in* feel excluded. Maybe it's the sorority of those who have children; of those whose parents are still living and well; or, of those who grew up with both parents in the home. Maybe it's the fraternity of those who went to college, who went to grad school, or who work in corporate America. It's whatever category you don't fit in; the thing that every now and again makes you feel set apart from others. The thing that makes you feel disconnected; like you're standing on the playground alone.

What's funny is that if we look around, we'll realize that everyone has things that make them feel different. The truth is, when we feel alone, it's really a big illusion.

We can focus on the things that differentiate us – whether they are permanent traits or temporary circumstances – and use it as a reason to isolate and retreat. (In my view, a fertile ground for depression.) Or, we can embrace the beauty of who we are, what it has taught us, and because of it who we've become.

Most importantly, we can remember that no matter what our circumstances, and no matter how we feel about them . . . we are never alone.

What About A Truce?

It wasn't nearly as hard as I'd expected.

Once I gave into the notion of working all weekend, and accepted that my business trip was going forward despite my prayers to the contrary, things actually went pretty smoothly. Acceptance gave me peace – kind of like I'd called a truce between where I want to be and where I am today. So, as I prepared for my work presentation, I actually found myself being okay with it. Though I might deny it later, there were certain parts I even enjoyed.

I focused on the positive of my work situation and found things to love about it: the people I work with are funny and they have real life balance. One of the partners has been married for over 40 years and still talks about his wife like she's a new bride. All in all, it's a fun group where I feel as if I can be myself.

So, maybe it's not such a bad thing if I find myself in this job for another year or two, right?

I don't know how to write in the long dramatic pause that followed that question. The truth is that this morning I'm feeling good and in a place of peace, except when I try to figure out this whole notion of letting go. Does letting go mean that I put my dreams on the back burner and embrace my day job in full? Does it mean that I let go completely of the thought of having a husband and/or kids? That I accept this present day reality in full and stop believing something else is around the corner? Where's the balance? And, after writing countless thoughts of the day, why does it seem that I'm still trying to get the same lesson?

The truth is that I'm scared. I'm scared because every time I've let go, I've looked up and a few years have passed with me seemingly in the same place. Then, I wonder why it feels as if I'm not making progress.

How do I keep my dreams – my desires – close enough so that I don't forget them; yet far enough that they aren't a constant reminder of what I don't currently have?

How do we put our prayers in the "something for Jesus to do" box, yet still ensure that we're taking steps in the between times in the right direction?

God says it's about faith. When we let go, part 1 of faith is trusting that God will work out our prayers at the perfect appointed time. Part 2 of faith is trusting ourselves; believing that if we remain prayerful, we'll keep taking steps – even if they are caterpillar steps – in the direction of our dreams. Even when it feels like we're moving in the wrong direction or not moving at all. As long as we remain prayerful, we've got to trust that the things we let go of – if they're meant for us – are coming back to us. Infinitely better than if we'd gotten them when we first asked.

My goal is to stop speaking badly about where I am in this very moment.

My goal is to stop making myself crazy by always wishing I was someplace else.

I will make the most of this moment, learn from it all I can, enjoy it to the fullest, and trust that even when I feel off course, there's a larger compass in play.

What About Happily Ever After?

Don't you love watching romantic movies where the guy and girl meet each other and they just know they were meant to be together? Sure, there may be a few obstacles during the one and a half hour film, but in the end, they ride off into the sunset.

Or, what about seeing Hollywood celebrities achieve some milestone? Like when Denzel won an Oscar for "Training Day." Or, when Oprah got her own television show.

Though I feel bad for admitting it, every now and again a twinge of "hateration" comes over me as I witness these events – even the fictitious ones. After all, poor me has been wanting to make a career change for several years. Poor me didn't get the happily after I dreamed of. Poor, poor me.

Ever felt that way?

Before I lose myself completely in my own story (which if I'm honest with myself is the story of a girl who has never in life had a need unmet), today I dug a little deeper and realized that my perspective may have been a tad bit skewed.

Denzel won an award after years of being passed over, including times when he made films that were in my opinion much better than "Training Day." God only knows how long it took him to get his first breakout role in a movie.

Oprah overcame a difficult childhood, the loss of a child, and many professional hurdles before she got her own show. Even then, she had to deal with issues regarding love, public struggles with her weight, and constant judgment of her every action.

The same is true for my movie characters. Even if they were real, I'm completely discounting what might have happened in the many years that preceded their happily ever after. There were probably real life curve balls from unexpected challenges that everyone has to face in life.

Perhaps next time we feel as if our fairytale is taking too long to manifest, we should remember that everyone has a road to walk before they get to the ever after.

What About The Mirror?

I've been struggling the past several days to put into words what I've been feeling. Nothing is particularly wrong, yet I find myself unexplainably back in a place of discontent.

My first notion, as always, was to point the finger outward toward the many potential 'culprits' in my life. I started with the usual suspects: job, family (my mom's health), relationships (or lack thereof), finances.... But, nothing produced an easy answer. No, I hadn't experienced any big break in these areas of my life; but at the same time, nothing was any worse either. So, you'd think there would be cause for celebration.

Except, I didn't feel like celebrating the fact that I was maintaining the status quo. That my job, family, relationships, and finances weren't any worse hardly seemed like enough to feel particularly good about.

I began to pray for guidance and peace. As often has been the case, the answer that came to me was not what I expected. The voice inside me simply said, "take a look in the mirror."

At first, I didn't understand. So, I continued to pray. Then, without completely understanding my destination, I walked over to my bookshelf and began pulling out journals from the past ten years. The more I read, the more I began to see myself and to understand.

I don't believe the past is for regrets. I believe the past is to teach us how to do and be better. As I read snippets of *my story*, I began to embrace the lessons I missed the first, second, and sometimes fifteenth time around. I realized that the discontent I feel is not so much because God hasn't moved in some area of my life; but instead, often times it's because I haven't moved when he told me to do so. In many instances, I've continued to move in the same circles.

My journal entries told of my undisciplined attempts to write and publish over the past decade, my **early** realization that my career was not a good fit, my repeated attempts to find the "right love" outside of me (instead of inside of me first), and my prayers for God to increase my financial territory (which he did, but then I similarly increased my spending). I realized that all of the things I've been praying to come to me have to first start inside of me.

When was the last time you looked in the mirror?

God, today I ask you to help me to see myself in full. Help me see the areas in my life where I need to change and grow; and give me the desire, strength, and discipline to do so. Help me learn the lessons so that I need not continue to repeat each course. As I work to do and be better, help me to love myself even more in my imperfections.

What About The Ups And Downs?

I feel dizzy.

After reading through some of my prior thoughts, I'm marveling at the emotional roller coaster of the past several months. Where is the optimistic, cool and confident woman I like to think of as myself? Does she get body-snatched or kidnapped when her evil twin starts talking about insecurities, fears, disappointments, and loneliness?

I used to think that one day I'd become this woman who never experienced any of those things. My peace would be so perfect that nothing in the world would ever shake me, and I would constantly be a beacon of light.

My quiet time with God has shown me that's not realistic. Why? Because I'm human, flawed, imperfect, and when it's all said and done, an emotional being. The fact that I love hard and am passionate about everything I do (or want to do) means that there will be times – from time to time – when I experience what a friend once called "divine discontent." Why? Because God made me in such a way that my quest is always for more and better. And, deep down, I believe that God made me for something special.

Aren't there moments when you feel that God placed you in this world to do something that only you can do? Don't you feel as if you owe it to yourself to keep working to uncover and attain that goal?

I do. It's my greatest motivation, and when I'm not feeling particularly strong, my greatest kryptonite. Knowing that I can and will be "more" drives me to do and be better, then makes me my worst critic. But, when I feel as if I'm missing the mark, it trickles into every other area of my life. It's a domino effect that, when I'm not careful, can leave me feeling as if I'm *so* far off track that I needn't keep trying. That feeling can plummet me to an all-time low.

It's like the man I met climbing Stone Mountain last week. He told me the story of how he was in great shape, took care of himself, and yet found himself facing a quadruple bypass at the age of 50. After the surgery, he thought "why bother" and stopped exercising, started smoking, and just became comfortable in a place of apathy.

As I heard his story, I realized that in some ways, he was a mirror of me. I am infamous for tapping in and doing what I know will push me toward the desires of my heart. I'll do a really good job until something shows me that despite my best efforts, I'm still not where I ultimately want to be. Then I exclaim "why bother?" and stop writing and exercising, start consuming toxic treats and proclaiming that my soulmate is never coming, and stop doing anything that will move me to a more rewarding career.

The man on the mountain stayed in his place of 'why bother' for several years before he had a startling realization. Something inside him stilled believed. Although his faith had been shaken by not having things move in the way he anticipated, he still believed. So, there he was, eight years after his bypass surgery. Back climbing the mountain. Back doing the things that he knew were right. Back giving it his all.

That man is me. I'm guessing that man might be you too.

So, today, let's make a pact. Let's not be discouraged if despite our best efforts, things don't seem to go our way. Let's not let any discouragement stop us from doing what we know needs to be done in order to be that special being God created. And, let's not be too hard on ourselves if there are days when we get off track, feel less balanced or doubt how special we really are.

After all, life is about ups and downs. We can't have one without the other. But, we can make the ups real tall mountaintops, and we can make the downs very slight declines, if we just keep moving forward, with our eyes on the prize.

What About Answers To Prayers?

Today is a beautiful day. Why? Because all of my prayers have been answered.

Now, before you go thinking that I 'drank the Kool-Aid,' let me just explain what I mean.

The past several months have been challenging. I've been praying for very specific breakthroughs in a few areas of my life. In fact, I was so diligent about it that I probably started sounding like I was giving a well rehearsed speech to God during my quiet time. Then, when I finished *telling* him exactly what I wanted – leaving no margin for error – I'd head off on my day, convinced that today would be the day that "X" would happen.

Well, you probably can imagine why I started getting pretty funky as the days turned to weeks, and the weeks turned to months, without me getting my "special order." At first, I got angry. But, that quickly dispelled when I looked around me and saw how many blessings I have. So, instead, I moved to a more familiar place. Stealing a line from Grey's Anatomy, I call it "the dark place."

Have you ever been in the dark place?

For me, the dark place is where I'm not happy or sad; I'm just resigned. I start saying things like "This is my life. This is my fate. So, let me stop fighting and just accept it. This is as good as it gets." Sometimes the dark place includes a full pity party – especially if your friends are singing about skittles and rainbows. But, most often you just walk around with an underlying hint of doom and gloom that shows that you'd rather be any place but in that moment.

Fortunately, I didn't stay in that place for long (which is good, because if you're not careful, it can get way too comfortable). Instead, I decided to find the root of my discontent.

My first thought: I'm upset because my prayers haven't been answered.

I turned that over and over in my mind, and probed a bit deeper. Then, it's almost like I felt God ask me, "Are you upset because I haven't answered your prayers, because you think I can't/won't answer them? Or, are you upset because I haven't answered your prayers in the way that you want . . . yet?"

Checkmate. (Playing chess with God is never fair!)

As I thought back, I realized that I was doing pretty well until I started with the specific, repetitious prayers that instead of bringing me peace, often reminded me that I was asking <u>again</u> because my prayers remained unanswered. In truth, I had (and have) no doubt that God will answer my prayers, just like always. I was just upset because I wanted it to be in my way, and in my time.

After more prayer, I stepped back and decided that since God undoubtedly remembered (from prayers 1-100) my specific requests, perhaps I should sometimes try a different approach for my daily prayers.

Instead of praying for a publishing deal and/or a new job, I prayed for God to keep me on purpose and to give me a joy so great that it wasn't dependent on any external circumstances.

Instead of praying for a mate, I prayed for abundant love, so that I wouldn't feel lonely.

Instead of praying for my mom to miraculously be healed, I prayed for her comfort and peace, and I prayed for God to give me an unselfish heart that keeps what's best for her prioritized above all else.

Instead of praying for a specific new source of income, I prayed for the wisdom and discipline to make good decisions that will provide for all my needs, many of my wants, and allow me to give abundantly.

At the end of the day, I realize that it's a lot simpler than I've been making it. Sure, I envision a specific way in which I want God to answer my prayers, but when it's all said and done, I really just want what everyone else does – love, joy, peace, purpose, and prosperity. And, when I ask God for these things, he never fails to provide.

What About Believing In Dreams?

Last weekend I was channel surfing and happened upon one of my favorite family movies, "Akeelah and the Bee." I flipped on just as Laurence Fishburne is telling Akeelah – who he describes as a "shrinking violet" – to read a quote by Marianne Williamson he has framed on the wall. The one that begins "Our deepest fear is not that we are inadequate."

After Akeelah finishes reading the quote, Laurence makes her boldly proclaim that in her heart of hearts, what she really wants is to win the National Spelling Bee. He reminds her that in order to do so, she just needs to fully believe she can.

I'm such a sap for touching movie scenes, so it probably comes as no surprise that this one makes my eyes water every time. It's more than the story of an 11 year old girl from the inner-city with a dream that seems larger than life. It's memories of myself as a little girl with a dream of writing books and touching lives. I remember how serious I was when I sat down with my pencil and large-lined paper to work on my first "best-seller." One of my earliest projects was a book to help parents understand the inner-thinking of a child. (Because I was convinced that parents just didn't get it!)

Can you imagine? I had to be about 10 or 11 at the time, and I thought I could write a book that would change the world.

But, even back then I was afraid. Afraid to think I was good enough to accomplish my goals, therefore afraid to admit that I had them. Afraid to believe that God could have given me a special gift – that I was talented enough to realize the dream I now know he placed in my heart. Afraid to believe . . . in me.

Have you ever been afraid to believe you can accomplish what God has placed in your heart?

I wish I could say a lot has changed in the last couple of decades, and I no longer have those fears. But, the truth is sometimes I'm still that little girl. The one who fears the dreams I have are too big or that I'm not special enough to achieve them.

Far too often, I ask myself: who am I to be brilliant, gorgeous, talented, and fabulous? Who am I to be a best-selling author?

But, the difference between me as an 11 year old little girl and me as a thirty-something year old woman is I finally know what to do when that question arises. When I find myself feeling uncertain, I tell that little gremlin voice to "shut it up" and I recognize it for the self-defeating, self-limiting, insecurity that it is. I recognize that it isn't a voice for my greater good, and remind myself that any dream God placed on my heart is just a future reality, waiting for me to be bold enough to reach out and grab it.

So, the next time you find yourself asking "who am I to be _____?" Go to the mirror, look yourself smack dead in the eyes, and ask,

"Who am I not to be?"

What About Stepping Out?

I've been holding onto my job out of fear. I self-righteously "preach" words to everyone else about God providing and God's will and not being afraid, but the truth of the matter is that I've probably been standing in my own way.

Every year around this time (right before annual evaluations), I forget everything I've said about wanting to walk into my purpose and destiny. I forget how much I've dreaded some aspects of my job, and how much I've prayed for a new beginning.

The same lips that uttered "please get me out of here," suddenly start to whisper "please help me keep this job." I remind God of how unprepared I am to step out on my own, and tell him that I need to finish executing my "freedom plan" first so that I have no bills and am ready to go without a struggle.

Honestly, if I'm real with myself, my goal was to be so prepared that I didn't need any faith to make it through. I wanted things to align in a way of certainty so there would be no fear, no insecurity, no struggle to figure out what's next. I wanted a plan that made it a sure thing.

This morning I realize that I've been holding on instead of telling God, "your will is supreme." Instead of telling God *how* I envision my move from here, I should trust him to make a way. Notwithstanding that a good job is hard to find. Notwithstanding that everyone says the economy sucks. Notwithstanding how unprepared I think I am.

Blessings sometimes come when you're willing to step outside the boat, without being able to see anything more than God's hand, promising that you won't have to walk on water alone.

Are you sitting in the boat out of fear today? Has God reached out his hand and told you that it's going to be okay, but you still don't believe?

Your boat could be anything you're holding onto for security – a job, a business, a relationship whose time has passed. Sometimes we've got to say, "I'm ready, God, for whatever you have for me, even if that means letting go of this thing that feels secure, but that I know is no longer right for me."

Today, it scares me to type these words, but I know it's time to do so. I hope you'll utter a similar prayer for anything in your life whose season has passed.

God, I release this job to you in full. In fact, I release everything in my life to you. I'm scared of the unknown and I don't have a clue how things will work out. Though I don't know what the future holds, the one thing I know for certain is that it's You who holds my hand. I also know that You will never let it go.

What About Wanting More?

"You need to be grateful that things aren't worse than what they are, or else God might show you how bad they can be."

I know what my mother intended to instill in me when she said these words, but somehow I think I got it a little twisted.

I was 15 years old and thought the world was coming to an end because I had this skin condition (psoriasis) that caused a temporary rash of sorts almost everywhere except my face, hands, and feet. As a teenager, I couldn't imagine anything worse than being a leper. So, I pouted and complained and had some "Why me, Lord?" moments that in hindsight seem hilarious, but at the time made perfect sense since life as I knew it had seemed to end.

My parents always tried to instill in me the notion of gratitude, and an understanding that things that came to me were blessings, not entitlements. That's why my mom thought it was a good idea to scare me into being more grateful. After all, if I wasn't, God might teach me a lesson.

I was 15 years old and thought the world was coming to an end because I had to wear long sleeve shirts throughout the spring while my rash and scars healed. Needless to say, I didn't feel very grateful.

Until the fall came, and right after my psoriasis healed, I found myself <u>completely</u> covered in blisters from head to toe with what I later learned was my <u>second</u> case of chicken pox. Since most folks only get chicken pox once, I was convinced that my mom's warning had been a real one. God was showing me who was boss, and had given me a taste of how bad things could really be. As I struggled with pox in my hair and under my feet (and everywhere in between), I swore that never again would I fail to give thanks for whatever situation came my way. The good, bad, and even the crazy. I don't even think I prayed for the chicken pox to go away. Instead, I thanked God from the bottom of my heart that it wasn't something worse or permanent, and tried to wait patiently for the season to pass.

As I meditate this morning, I realize that it makes perfect sense that two decades later, I struggle from time to time when I want to pray for certain things in my life. I look at the fact that I've been blessed with a family that's given me more love than some folks are blessed with in a lifetime, and I think that maybe it's asking too much to request more quality time with my mom. I think that with all the love in my life, maybe I should be grateful for what I have instead of praying for romantic love too.

I look at the job that has given me material comforts, and think maybe I shouldn't complain about the things I don't like about it. Maybe it's enough that I'm able to take care of my needs and many wants. After all, it could always be worse.

I observe myself running and moving and doing things that some folks with infirmities can't do, and I stop whining when I get a migraine or don't feel in perfect health.

Today was the first time that I realized that there's a part of me – a little tiny piece – that is afraid to "push my luck." After all, I need to be grateful for what I have, lest God show me how bad it can really get. Right?

Have you ever been afraid to ask God for more? Thought that you should just be glad things aren't worse – and maybe even decided to accept good enough, instead of praying for great?

I have. As if I don't know and believe that God is the source of abundance and prosperity of all types. As if God is spiteful and petty, waiting in the wings to take away my blessings because I dared to be discontent with what I have, and had the nerve to want more.

Don't get me wrong; I know what my mom was trying to teach me. Tomorrow isn't promised. Love, perfect health, prosperity, joy – all of these things are gifts that are precious, for which we should be grateful.

I get that.

Yet, I don't think God wants us to be afraid to be discontent with what we've been given. I don't think he meant for us to be shackled to situations that are good enough, but not great. I don't think that wanting more in our lives is ever a slap in the face to him. If anything, I think it's more offensive when we don't ask for the desires he's placed on our hearts; when we don't believe in the miracles large and small that are within a prayers reach.

This morning, I'm looking at the things in my life that could be better. Though I know they could always be worse, and though I'm thankful for the many blessings, I'm daring to ask God for what I *really* want.

How about you?

What About Waiting On Prayers To Be Answered?

I must admit that I almost erased this entry shortly after writing it. My thought? No one wants to hear the same old whining about you waiting on prayers to be answered. Been there. Done that. Get over it already.

But, the truth of the matter is that no matter how much peace I gain, no matter how happy I am, and no matter how easily I've learned to regain my peace and happiness when they try to escape me; I still have days when I feel some discontent with where I am. I guess it's just a symptom of being human.

This morning what struck me is that several years ago I had a dream about my writing that showed me I was supposed to write about my life. I knew without a shadow of a doubt that if I did my part, God would give me a successful writing career. I didn't understand how it would come to fruition, but I knew it was more than a dream – it was a vision.

Okay, does any part of that first sentence stick out to you? Let's read it again.

"SEVERAL YEARS AGO, I had this dream about my writing that showed me I was supposed to write about my life."

YEARS!

Yep, after having that dream, it took me at least 4 years to "get ready" to write. Another 3 years for me to finish even one manuscript. Then, of course, for the last year I've been shopping my writing to publishers, while continuing to write and edit. Alternating between waiting on the phone to ring with "the call" and trying to forget about it so I don't end up in a place of discontent.

SEVERAL YEARS later and I'm still praying for that dream to become a reality. Most days I'm patient, knowing that everything happens at the perfect anointed time. But, on those not so great days, I find myself wondering if and when it will happen. And, on some other days – even when I'm sure that it's coming – I still get tired of waiting.

Have you ever waited on a prayer to be answered? I mean, you prayed about your desires to make sure they were the right ones, made your request known to God, and then believed with faith that could move mountains? Yet, the mountain didn't move?

Every time I get to this place, I find myself wondering if there's some piece of the puzzle that I'm missing. Wondering if there's something more I should be doing. Wondering if my desires aren't in the right place, or if my faith isn't as strong as I think it is. After all, if all those things line up, there shouldn't be any hold up, right?

I almost didn't write this message today because the questions I'm asking aren't anything new. But, I know that God placed this on my heart because maybe there's at least one person who at this very moment needs to be reminded that sometimes dreams take time. That doesn't make the vision you received any less real. It just means that you've got to make peace with this preparatory phase that you're in, embrace it, and enjoy each and every moment while knowing that your dreams are being realized each and every day. And, sometimes when you stop and get perspective, you might just find that you're already living a piece of the dream. After all, I am writing about my life, just as I envisioned. Well, except for the "real job" that supports me, and minus the "O" bookclub imprint.

So, in spite of my hesitations with writing the same old message again, I'm writing this today to tell you that if there's something that you've been praying on that hasn't yet come to pass, don't give up. Your mountain is moving. Even when you're too tired to pray that it will. Especially when you're too tired to hope that it will.

Trust.

What About Keeping On?

I just woke up from the strangest dream. I was in a large hotel room with a group of folks. Some of them I recognized as attorneys from my firm; others I'd never seen before. Most of the members of the group held instruments. As my colleague counted them in, the group began to play.

It was a pretty bad version of the song "Heaven," which quickly got tossed to the side for another tune. Despite the awful playing, I found myself smiling and energized as I thought, "Now this is more like it!"

Somewhere between sleep and waking, I realized that I like many of the people that I work with, as well as other things about my job. I just know – even in my dreams – that I should be working in the arts. Anything less feels like I'm suffocating.

Have you ever known down to the core that you should be someplace other than where you are?

I feel that way every day, 80% of the time that I'm in that office. I go through the motions, while dreaming of something better coming along. I comb the job ads, unsure what I'm looking for; and sometimes even play the lotto with hopes of a win.

The only problem is, even though I know this isn't where I'm supposed to be, I can't quite figure out my next move. I want to write; that much is clear; but I also want to eat. I just haven't yet figured out how to do both.

This morning I prayed about what to do; about what my next move should be; about whether I should make some radical move. I waited for God to give me some profound answer. But, what I heard was more simple than I could have ever imagined.

God said "just keep writing."

Whatever it is that God placed on your heart to do, just keep doing it and know that he's preparing the place for you. You just keep doing that thing that feels right to your spirit and the path will be cleared for you. Just don't stop!

If you don't yet know what that thing is, that's ok! Sometimes you're halfway there before you realize where you're going. Have faith that you're doing "it" and faith that when "it" blossoms, it will be something beautiful.

What About Feeling Alone?

Am I the only one whose dreams have soundtracks? I woke up this morning to the tune of Toni Tone singing "Just me and you . . . you don't need nobody else." (I don't question the muse's choice, I just groove to it!)

I lay there in the stillness of the early morning, and at some point became aware that I was smiling to myself. When I thought about it more, I recognized that my smile came from the realization that I'd turned an old R&B song into gospel. Somehow, I'd transposed the words into a song that was just for me and God.

Who would have ever thought when I started this journey that I'd be excited about my morning moments? That I'd find myself looking forward to getting up, instead of struggling in the way I did in the first weeks?

What's more, who would have thought when I started this journey that I'd be excited about God being the one with whom I can share everything? The one who I tell my dreams and disappointments, and who I look to for comfort and peace? I guess that's what I should have been doing all along, but I have to say that my track record was kind of spotty.

Now that I'm in a better place, I have a confession to make. When my mom's illness began to progress, I found myself questioning where I fit into the big scheme of things. For as long as I can remember, my identity has been associated with who I belong to. I was "one of Rutha Mae's girls." Then I swapped that identity to become somebody's wife. Then, when my marriage didn't work out as planned, I quickly found home again as "one of Rutha Mae's girls."

That's how it's always been.

Perhaps you can imagine my fear and discomfort when I woke up one day and realized my mother's impending mortality. I found myself questioning who I'll be when my mother transitions, and who I'll belong to then.

As a mostly confident and secure woman (despite my moments to suggest otherwise), I was really disturbed by the notion that I needed anyone else to define me. And, since I'd long ago learned the difference between "alone" and "lonely," I couldn't even process what I was feeling. I found myself asking, is this what it feels like to be lonely?

Have you ever felt that way? Like though you were in a sea of people, somehow you were still all alone?

I started praying then. I told God that I was tired of being so independent, tired of doing it all alone. I wanted to feel safe, secure, protected, provided for and, of course, loved.

When I prayed, I envisioned the answer to my prayers. Though the physical appearance in my vision often changed, the spirit of my imagined soulmate was always the same.

Except, I forgot that God doesn't always answer prayers literally. Instead, he gives us what we need, in spite of ourselves. And, he has a huge sense of humor (that I don't always appreciate in the moment).

So, I'm laughing this morning as I realize that somewhere along the way during this journey, I've gotten what I asked for. Although I must laugh at how my "soulmate" appeared.

He isn't exactly tall, dark and handsome in the way that I envisioned. But, with him, I feel safe, secure, protected, provided for . ... and more loved than ever before. Plus, the best part is that my identity will never change because I'll always be part of him. (Just like I'll always be "one of Rutha Mae's girls.")

I've learned there will be times in life when no matter how many mates, children, family members, and friends you have, you may feel alone. But, I've realized that those aren't the times to reach out. Instead, those are the times to reach in. Strangely enough, that's where you'll find everything you need.

Next time God puts you in a place where it feels like just you and him, resist the natural inclination to believe you need anything or anyone else. Maybe, just maybe, your place of solitude could be your greatest source of refuge, growth, and strength.

God, I thank you for the times when it's just me and you. I thank you for giving me more love than I could ever return and for being a constant source of peace and security. I thank you that with you, I need never feel alone. And, most of all, that I never have to be lonely.

Acknowledgements

I thank God for waking me on mornings when I didn't want to get up, giving me the right words when I personally didn't have anything to say, and for keeping me moving forward when I didn't have a real vision for what was to come.

Now I understand that I had to write early in the morning because that's the only time when I wouldn't have gotten in my own way. Any other time I would have been second-guessing each word and trying to make it my perfect masterpiece. Instead, in the early morning hour, I was a blank slate for God to create on. Wouldn't it be wonderful if we learned to be like this in all ways?

I am thankful that this tiny, independent project – that began with a short email distribution list – is going to be life-changing for someone. If no one else, my life has surely been changed in writing it.

There are so many family members and friends who I should probably thank for helping me get to this point – who encouraged me, supported me, invested in me, and threatened me when I didn't send messages for weeks at a time – but, I hope they'll all forgive me as I instead give my full and eternal gratitude to my mother.

Several weeks before I finished this book, my mom began to speak in a way that people often do before they transition. She talked to my sister and me about her love for us and gave us advice such as "always stick together" in the future.

After I thought she had finished speaking, she looked at me in a way that I couldn't decipher. Her eyes watered as she told me of her fear (because of my relatively young age) that I hadn't gotten enough time with her and my dad, who died when I was 17.

My heart momentarily grew heavy, and I struggled with how to respond. Then I smiled at her and spoke truth. I told her that she'd given me more love in my 37 years than some people know in their entire lifetimes.

I thank God for giving me a mother who personified his love so beautifully, who taught me how to love myself, and whose legend will live on through all of those who she sowed love into, for now and forever more.

I love you mommy.

Made in the USA
Lexington, KY
18 June 2010